At Home – Charleston

TRADITIONS AND ENTERTAINING
IN A CHARLESTON HOME

By Catherine H. Forrester

Charleston, South Carolina

With a Foreword by
Nathalie Dupree

Edited by
Barbara G. S. Hagerty

Photographs by
Jack Alterman

At Home ~ Charleston

TRADITIONS AND ENTERTAINING
IN A CHARLESTON HOME

Library of Congress Catalog Number: 2005911409

ISBN 0-9776010-0-5

Manufactured in the United States of America

First Printing 2006   5,000 copies

WIMMER
COOKBOOKS

A CONSOLIDATED GRAPHICS COMPANY

800.548.2537   wimmerco.com

Dedication

In loving memory of my grandmother, Juliette Wiles Staats, who shared with me her beauty, grace, and affection, and her fascination with the world, and who taught me to pass them on through food and entertaining—

and to my grandfather, Henry Philip Staats, who through his vision and his training in architecture and preservation left an important legacy to the city he loved, and who instilled in me an appreciation of the rural landscapes that surround us.

Acknowledgements

This book moved from fantasy to reality only because of the constant support of the people in my life. My greatest thanks go to my children, Catherine Staats Forrester and John Ruston Forrester, and my lifelong friend Susan Tucker Rindal, all of whom believed in the idea, and never stopped encouraging me to pursue it.

Without the memories of my mother, Juliette Gay Staats Huffman, there would have been many holes in the stories I have told. My father, Robert Huffman, and my brothers, Phil and Jim Huffman, also added their memories and anecdotes as the chapters began to unfold. I am grateful for their support.

To my mentors and cheerleaders, Nathalie Dupree and Barbara Hagerty, I would never have pursued this project had it not been for the encouragement of "real" writers. Nathalie—when I spent the week with you at Rich's Cooking School in 1980, I never dreamed that our paths would cross again twenty-some years later, and that you would have such confidence that this project could come to fruition. To Barbara—a special thank you for your thoughtful editing. Your perspective as a true Charlestonian, your understanding of the ethos of this story, and your skill as an editor turned the recollections of an amateur into a poignant memoir.

I also owe thanks to the many friends, relatives, and colleagues who tasted and tested along the way. To my friend, Cozy Pelzer, who encouraged my endeavors and shared her sense of style and her memories of my grandmother, thank you. I remain grateful to my boss, Dana Beach, for his years of encouragement and advice and for allowing me the flexibility in my day job to complete this project. I would be remiss if I did not thank all my colleagues at the Coastal Conservation League for their roles as cheerleaders, testers, and tasters. They always enjoyed the samples—even the mistakes! I owe a special thanks to Heather Spires whose support throughout the project and eye for detailed copy-editing enhanced the finished product.

Jack Alterman helped me share my vision through his beautiful photographs, and Janet Gregg, Marian Small, and Kit Bennett enlivened each scene with fresh flowers and an eye for aesthetics. My thanks go also to Laura and Steve Gates who allowed us to photograph the country picnic at their serene piece of the world on Wadmalaw Island.

Finally, I am indebted to the many friends and family who visited my grandparents and who shared their stories of parties, of favorite recipes, and of Charleston in another time.

Foreword

Once upon a time in glorious Charleston—and, really, not so very long ago—a style of living, cooking, and entertaining was practiced that epitomizes and, some might say, defines the very heart and soul of graciousness. Nowhere in that grand old city was the art of hospitality more beautifully and artfully practiced than at the home of Juliette Wiles Staats, perhaps Charleston's quintessential hostess from the early 1940s until the late 1980s.

Now Mrs. Staats' granddaughter, Cathy Forrester, has written an enchanting book which, through its narrative and photographs, takes us behind those high, fabled walls to provide a rare and intimate look at the art of entertaining as it was conducted at one special Charleston residence. *At Home ~ Charleston* takes us behind the scenes in a very private home in a very private city and provides an intimate—and unprecedented—portrait of a style of entertaining which is now, sadly, almost gone with the wind!

For today's visitors to the city—and perhaps indeed for its residents as well—it is difficult to imagine that not so long ago Charleston was known as "America's Best Kept Secret." This book takes us back to those slower days and to an era when hostesses were willing—and able—to expend almost unlimited time and effort to make sure their guests were pampered. It provides a tantalizing glimpse into the traditions, customs, and gracious lifestyle that have lured visitors and transplants to the historic city for generations.

Enhancing the book are quotations from noted Charleston authors, anecdotes from Mrs. Staats' correspondence, and pages from the "party books" she so meticulously kept. Written in her elegant long-hand, the pages describe the menu, guests, and table settings for each event, from simple suppers at home to her signature black-tie dinner parties for thirty. They also reveal a charming and witty woman who throughout her long life remained forever intrigued by people, and who relished the opportunity to entertain and to share the private rooms of her historic house and garden.

These recipes—handed down through generations and honed during a lifetime of entertaining—are timeless. As usable today as yesterday, they have been tested and retested both by grandmother in her role of hostess and by granddaughter in her role of archivist and scribe.

There is no other book quite like *At Home ~ Charleston*. Both cookbook and memoir, it grants a rare, insider's view of a private style of living and entertaining that we are rapidly losing. It is as close to time-traveling as I can imagine—both for those who know Charleston and those who have yet to meet her.

~ NATHALIE DUPREE
TV Host and
Cookbook Author

At Home ~ Charleston

Traditions and Entertaining in a Charleston Home

TABLE OF CONTENTS

CHAPTER I
MY GRANDMOTHER'S RECEIPT BOOKS

I have over 400 cookbooks. I've counted them. Some are new, with beautiful glossy photographs of gorgeous food in exotic locales. Some are old, their pages tattered and yellowed. Some are French classics, by such masters as Escoffier and Julia Child. Some, like *Culture and Cuisine* and *Food in History,* are fascinating references. Some are regional; some are ethnic. And some—like the seductive writings of M.F.K. Fisher—are part memoir. Some I use often; they line the shelves in my kitchen. Others—many passed down by my grandmother—fill eight shelves in my small study.

But my most treasured "receipts" (the charming, old-fashioned term for recipes, still in use in some Charleston households) aren't in the books. They reside in the numerous small boxes of index cards; in a frayed, black loose-leaf notebook; and especially in the pages of a small, sage-green book called *A Cookbook for Gay.* In 1949, a year before my mother, Juliette Gay Staats, was married, my grandmother, Juliette Wiles Staats, assembled and self-published the small book filled with favorite family recipes. The inside cover states, "Price one dollar," but to the best of my knowledge the book was never actually sold. Instead, it was given away to friends and relatives over many decades. When I was a child we often gave a copy of the book to a favorite teacher at the end of the school year. Even today friends and acquaintances will ask if they can have a new copy because theirs is too stained or worn to read, or because they have a child getting married. Frequently, people tell me of a particular recipe in the cookbook which was a family favorite and always made on special occasions. When they hear about this book, they say, "Oh, I hope you are going to include that recipe!"

In later years, my grandmother and I would always add a minor correction or two when giving the books away. A number of years ago, encouraged by my mother, I thought I might rewrite the book both to correct those inaccuracies and to add a number of family favorites which had not originally been included. Another goal has been to standardize the recipes themselves. "Add butter the size of a walnut, mix as for any cake, and bake in the oven until done" is hardly a complete recipe by today's standards. In her book *Food in History,* Reay Tannahill writes that it was *The Boston Cooking School Cookbook*—first published in 1896, and generally known eponymously by the name of its author, Fannie Farmer—which initiated the standardization of recipes we know today. Prior to that, measurements such as "a pinch of salt," "a nut of butter," or "a wine glass of brandy" were commonplace. In fact, in the front of my family notebook of recipes is a list of equivalents, that translates for today's cook such arcane measurements as a wine glass, a liqueur glass, a sherry glass, and a pony glass.

In the fifth edition of *The Carolina Housewife,* first published in 1847, the preface relates the disasters that can occur when "that notoriously thoughtless person—the husband" brings dinner guests home unexpectedly. It continues:

> *Much of the discomfort of this might be spared were our grandmother's receipt-books so studied as to make it easy to teach the cook to send up the simplest meal properly dressed, and good of its kind. But the manuscript, in which is gathered a whole lifetime's experience, cannot be in the possession of more than one family in ten. It rarely happens that more than one woman in three generations takes the pains to collect and arrange receipts; and if her descendants are many, the greater part lose the benefit of her instructions.*

How fortunate my family is that my grandmother was one of those who took the pains to collect and arrange the recipes handed down through generations, for they record a familial and cultural history, and continue to bring joy to many.

As I thought more about this project, it occurred to me that my family, those who knew my grandmother, and anyone who loves Charleston would enjoy a book that included not only the recipes but also photographs of the house and garden and vignettes

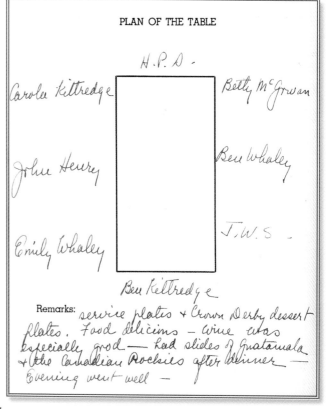

Where given *at home Charleston* Date *Jan. 23/60*

Occasion *Dinner*

Guests Present

Mr. & Mrs. Ben Kittredge
Mr. & Mrs. Ben Scott Whaley
Mrs. Elizabeth McGowan
Mr. John Henry Dick

Unable to Attend

Menu

Green turtle soup
veal scallopini
watercress —
rice ring
fresh green beans
Creme brulée with
brandied apricots
Demi-tasse

Wines
Chateau Olivier
1952
(a delicious graves given us by Mrs. H. Phipps.)

Table Decorations apricot + white damask cloth — silver candlesticks — blue glass + silver compotes + salt dishes etc. — amethyst glass — blue + red

PLAN OF THE TABLE

H.P.D. —

Carola Kittredge   Betty McGowan

John Henry   Ben Whaley

                                    J.W.S. —

Emily Whaley

Ben Kittredge

Remarks: service plates + Crown Derby dessert plates. Food delicious — wine was especially good — had slides of Guatemala + the Canadian Rockies after dinner — Evening went well —

about Gran's life and style of entertaining. For in many ways Gran was an artist, and entertaining in all its facets—bringing people together, setting an artful table, conjuring a convivial atmosphere, and presenting superb food—was her medium, just as a sculptor's medium may be marble or a painter's oil. Unlike today's shortcut-prone hostesses, Gran thought nothing of having major furniture moved out of the way to accommodate the round tables and chairs needed for a seated dinner party, or of spending ten days in pursuit of the perfect beef suet for her Christmas puddings. For several years I wrote the book in my head whenever I was cooking, thinking of the occasions when my grandmother prepared the same recipes, the parties at which they were served, and the stories she told about their origins.

Stored with all Gran's cookbooks and file cards are her party books. These six beautiful, leather-bound volumes made by Mark Cross record—beginning Christmas, 1955, and ending December, 1987—the guests, those unable to attend, seating arrangements, table decorations and, of course, menu and wines served. Next to the entry "Where Given" is noted most frequently *At Home ~ Charleston.* These books—recorded in her old-fashioned longhand, in the blue ink of her fountain pen—are not only a unique record of a manner of entertaining that is rare today but also a social history of Charleston. Gran's guest lists often included notable Charlestonians from the mid-twentieth century, such as writers Josephine Pinckney and Paul Hyde Bonner; artists John Henry Dick and Elizabeth O'Neill Verner; preservationists Bob and Patty Whitelaw and Dorothy Legge; and neighbor Emily Whaley, who became famous several years ago for her books on gardening and entertaining. They are all scattered through the pages along with house guests from "Off" and numerous other Charleston characters. Nearly all of them were members of a generation whose way of life—for better *and* worse—is no longer.

Most of the menus and recipes you will find in this book were served at my grandmother's parties; many of them are recipes that were handed down for generations in her family. You will not find many recipes for hors d'oeuvres. As my grandmother told me, "If I'm going to go to all the trouble to cook a nice dinner, I don't want my guests to spoil their appetites before they ever get to the table." Indeed, at her supper parties, cocktails in the formal, second-floor drawing room began promptly at seven o'clock. Usually, just light hors d'oeuvres were offered: salted pecans; thin, salted bennes (a wafer made from the benne seed, or wild sesame, brought to these shores by African slaves); or piquant cheese straws, a Charleston tradition. Guests were called downstairs to dinner promptly at seven forty-five. The modern tendency of guests to arrive thirty minutes later than invited, or of hosts to allow two hours of cocktails before serving dinner, was not the modus operandi on Church Street (a schedule which caught more than one guest by surprise).

Equally on a par with the food was the company. Inside her first party book, she taped an unattributed quotation that reads in part, "I'd settle for a little less fuss over the food and drink and a little more forethought to the company." Parties were an occasion not just for enjoying good food but also—and perhaps more importantly—assembling interesting mixes of people and stimulating lively conversation. So the guest list and the seating arrangement (duly noted in the party book) received every bit as much thought as the menu selection. In another party book, Gran tucked a quote (which her note in the margin attributes to "Observations of a Chinese in America") that stated, "A cocktail party is one at which one attains the maximum physical movement with the minimum mental activity. It is also a place where you talk with a person you do not know about a subject in which you have no interest." Needless to say, my grandmother rarely gave cocktail parties. She was fascinated by people, and how could one have any sort of meaningful conversation at a cocktail party?

> *It is also my fault that I enjoy having people in my house, and so I make an effort, and often find it more of an effort than I anticipated. But I am not very sympathetic with people who have a sweep-out once a year at the Yacht Club—a cocktail party. Some Charlestonians do have the sweep-outs at their own home, but I doubt if they can even speak to all their guests, such as the party I recently went to. We did meet the guest of honor, but did not even see our host.*
>
> ~JWS – 11/3/1976

In addition to my grandmother's menus, I have included some additional ones that I have assembled from her recipes. At the back of the book, I have added a number of other recipes which have become family favorites: some are hers and some have come to me from other sources. In her later years, my grandmother referred to herself as "Great Aunt Maude." By that she meant that she had lived long enough to have attained both a certain wisdom and the liberty that age confers to speak her mind. But it also meant that she was the touchstone for many branches and generations of the family, some of whom she had never actually met. Over a number of decades, she researched and recorded the genealogies of the Staats and Wiles branches of the families. She was also an inveterate letter writer, sending hundreds of letters to my mother over the years. These, thankfully, Mother kept; they are oft-quoted in the following pages. The genealogies she recorded, the stories she told, the notebooks she kept, the letters she wrote, and the recipes she wrote down preserve the history and memories of many generations.

I like to think that I'm still a bit young to be the next Great Aunt Maude. But I am flattered to share the mantle of caretaker of these recipes. I enjoy being the one who follows her traditions: making the homemade jams in the summer, the caramel cake for birthdays, and the pumpkin pie and plum pudding for the holidays. I also have the privilege of living in her house, which is very much as she left it. I use the same linens, porcelains, and silver that Gran used; I cut flowers for the table from the same vines and shrubs that she once did. So if you have known Gran as family, friend, or house guest, if you have visited her house, or if you want a glimpse of a way of life which, in Charleston as elsewhere, is fast disappearing, I hope you will find some pleasure in these pages.

Henry Philip Staats and Juliette Wiles Staats ~Rio, 1939

Chapter II
Privacy, Integrity, and Change

I remember old Daisy, the horse at Aunt Nellie's, hitched to the buggy and brought around each morning so that we could go to the market—and that was a man with a flat wagon, full of fresh farm produce. Then my father who had one of the very first automobiles, with only rare paved roads, mostly brick in the larger towns. And now this great web of super highways all over this country. I have seen all of that. And then almost the end of ships for travel, and telephones to every part of the world; the incredible progress in medicine and drugs; and the airplanes. Being on the old DeGrasse when Lindberg flew across the Atlantic; making one of the first trans-Atlantic flights, huddled in blankets, no heat, coming down for gasoline and for meals; no trays and drinks and such, and always flying at certain altitudes because of lack of pressurized cabins, and on and on and on. Aunt Nellie's kitchen with its wood-burning stove. Think of electric ranges, microwave ovens, freezers, and the whole field of frozen foods; with refrigeration, the shipping of perishable foods all over the country, and the explorations of the world and the heavens, and men landing on the moon and being returned safely to earth. Is it any wonder that my mind flits in awe all over the place? And I would dearly love to have some depth of understanding of these and many other things too numerous to mention. It has been one of the most fabulous periods in all of history to be alive.

~ JWS – 11/11/80

Juliette Wiles ~ age 8

My grandmother, Juliette McCague Wiles, was born in 1906 in Ripley, Ohio. Her ancestors had been some of the earliest settlers in Brown County, Ohio, moving there from Pennsylvania in the first decade of the nineteenth century. Gran's grandmother, Juliette Burnham Hathaway Wiles, was one of a long line of adventurous women. She had initially been schooled at Granville Female Seminary in Ohio (now Denison University), but learned at the end of her second year that Antioch College was to become coeducational under the great educator, Horace Mann. Her stepfather, who strongly believed in education for women, gave his permission for her to transfer, and in 1852 Miss Hathaway entered Antioch, where she would meet her future husband, Newton Paine Wiles.

Juliette Hathaway Wiles went on to become an active civic leader, making speeches, dressing in the latest style, and leading many local organizations. She became the head of the Women's Christian Temperance Union in Ripley, although she always made wine, brandied peaches, and other dishes which included spirits. At one point she was asked to give the welcoming address when the state W.C.T.U. met in Ripley. Afterwards, when her husband complimented her on her speech, she replied, "Well, Newton, that drink of whiskey you gave me before I went helped a lot!"

In 1910, Gran and her family moved to Huntington, West Virginia, where several years later her father was elected mayor. She had three younger brothers—Luther, Kirk, and Leon. They remained close to their grandparents and cousins on both the West Virginia and Ohio sides of the Ohio River. Gran often told me about aunts, cousins, and neighbors of hers who were wonderful cooks. Aunt Nellie, skilled at dealing with the challenges of baking in a wood-burning oven, had only to "put her hand in the oven to know when it was the right temperature to bake her cake." Cousin Corinne made the wonderful Kentucky Cream Candy. Mrs. Meek from Huntington made delicious cakes; Mrs. Gwinn, also from Huntington, "had cream that rolled back like velvet." Many family and friends had longtime hired cooks such as Gertrude, Mamie, Mary, and Myrtle; numerous recipes come from them. These names and others—along with an occasional brief remembrance about an individual cook or her recipe—are scattered through my collection of old recipes.

Reminiscences of Juliette Belle Kirker Gregg, sent to her first cousin, Juliette Wiles Staats, in letters in the 1940s and 1960s, give a glimpse of family life, traditions, and recipes from their grandparents' home:

> *The rising bell rung at 7:00 a.m....the breakfast bell rung at 7:30, and you better be down there for breakfast with Grandpa standing at the head of the table, and we all stood while he asked grace. The huge breakfasts, and no one got fat. Why?*

Cousin Juliette goes on to remember that she walked a mile to school (returning home for lunch and going back to school for afternoon classes, a daily total of four miles), which no doubt burned off those huge breakfasts.

> *The baked beans, pickled pigs feet, head cheese, jams, jellies, home-made sauerkraut, the dark and light fruit cakes and hickory nut cakes and pound cake and home-made candies molded by hand and hidden in the back parlor where I sneaked in and stole pieces, carefully rearranging them so no one could tell I had done it. All the family from everywhere coming for dinner (dozens of people), a big turkey at each end of the table, with the bell ringing to call us to dinner...The pancakes and cornbread and Woodford pudding; the fresh sausage and sorghum from the Stephenson farm each fall...*

Throughout these letters and notes runs a recurrent theme: that food and recipes, handed down through the generations, played an important role in family gatherings. Perhaps it is this very adherence to tradition that made Gran's entertaining so appealing. For Gran's menus always—despite trends and innovations in food and styles of cooking—featured recipes that were traditional and tasty, rather than trendy.

When Gran was fourteen, her father died in the Spanish flu pandemic. Her mother, Granny Wiles, did something that must have been very unusual in 1918 for a widow with four children: she closed up the house in Huntington and began a multi-year sojourn, moving around the country and finally alighting in France. They lived for a short time on the California coast in La Jolla, just north of San Diego. The following year they rented a house on Wilshire Boulevard, which at that time was in the country outside the young city of Los Angeles. But the location I heard most about was Antibes in the south of France. There they rented the *Villa Champ Tercier* and settled in for a year, from 1925 to 1926.

In Antibes, my grandmother (now age nineteen), her mother, and younger brothers became part of the American expatriate colony. That was the Jazz Age; the expatriate experience for Americans was in full flower. Two novelists, F. Scott Fitzgerald and Ernest Hemingway, were to record it in several immortal works of fiction, including *Tender is the Night* and *The Sun Also Rises*.

Gran and her family walked from the hilltop villa down into the small town of Antibes for their shopping, returning by horse and carriage. Tea dances were the fashion for young ladies at the time, and my grandmother attended many of them. Evenings might mean dinner at the casino in Juan-les-Pins, or a private party in the villa of another of the American expatriates. Gran used to fascinate me with her stories of F. Scott Fitzgerald coming to tea, or of Ernest Hemingway pushing his bicycle down the village streets.

An entry in the diary of Gran's Aunt Bay Kirkpatrick, who visited Antibes with her daughters in 1926, gives a flavor of their life there:

Juliette Wiles (second from right) with her brothers and cousins ~ Antibes, France, 1926

A Mr. and Mrs. Adams, with artists, gave a costume dinner and ball and <u>never</u> have I attended such an interesting "peppy" party. A variety of people represented, artists, writers, actresses, officials, young and less young. Judy [Gran] and Dorothy went as boys. Luther dressed as a beach girl and A.J. as a very small girl wearing a dress of Anne's and a hair ribbon and carrying a doll. All four were original and cute. It was to have been a garden dinner but almost at the moment invited for, a storm descended, so instead of dinner first, then dancing, the order was reversed. So impressed by the easy casual manner of the Adams, undisturbed by any change in plans. The dancer in "No, No, Nanette" gave a clever solo stunt. Laura and I who were "audience" had something of interest to watch every moment. Too much drinking indulged in by some. From a long table out of doors food was served at twelve. Our children had made some most amusing remarks over late appearance of same. We left the party at one, the first ones to leave as it continued until about morning. I enjoyed meeting the handsome F. Scott Fitzgerald, writer.

During their year in France, Gran ventured even further afield, traveling with her younger brother Luther, elderly Aunt Nellie Kirker, and family friend Mrs. North, to North Africa. Riding sidesaddle on camels, the old ladies in their black dresses, Gran in her 1920's flapper-style chemise, and young Luther in a fez must have made quite a sight!

As that year drew to a close, the Wiles had a visit from a former West Virginia neighbor, Perry Duncan, who, having just graduated from Yale with a degree in architecture, was touring France and Italy with his classmate, Phil Staats. For the rest of her life, my grandmother would say, "I met your grandfather when he and Perry Duncan

Juliette Wiles (second rider from left) in North Africa, 1926

were backing up the hills of Italy." It seems that the availability of petrol for their Model T was somewhat unreliable in the European countryside, and the young men kept spare gas in wine bottles with rags stuffed into the necks. When fuel was low, they backed up the hills so that gravity would ensure an adequate supply to the car's engine. The story is that as the young men drove up the drive toward the *Villa Champ Tercier*, my grandfather looked up and saw my grandmother sitting in the window, brushing her long dark hair, and fell in love with her instantly.

Born in 1900, Henry Philip Staats hailed from an old New York family. His ancestors, having settled along the Hudson River at Ft. Orange (now Albany) in 1642, were among the first Dutch families in New Amsterdam. In 1927, after my grandparents were married in Lake Placid, New York, they embarked on a six-month honeymoon, which culminated in a year spent in Montecito, California, just south of Santa Barbara. There, my grandfather practiced architecture and authored a book on local

Henry Philip Staats ~ Antibes, France, 1926

architecture, *Californian Architecture in Santa Barbara*, which was published in 1929 and reissued in 1990. It was in Montecito that my mother was born.

All her married life, Gran loved to cook and spend time in the kitchen. Coming from a family with such a heritage of food, cooking, and recipes, it was almost her birthright. There was one notable hiatus, however, in this routine. Early in her marriage, they lived briefly with her husband's mother in a large, East Side New York apartment. There, her stern and very formal mother-in-law, Marie Hallenbeck Staats, forbade her to set foot in the kitchen! This ban must have come, no doubt, as quite a shock to my grandmother. As the years passed, however, and my grandparents established their own homes in Connecticut and later in Charleston, Gran pursued her love of cooking and entertaining. In her younger years, when they lived in the northeast, she took many cooking lessons from the well-known Dione Lucas, an Englishwoman who was the first female graduate of Le Cordon Bleu cooking school in Paris. She also attended classes held at "Au Gourmet" at Bloomingdale's in New York, which were taught by top Manhattan chefs. I still have some of the recipe booklets she kept from those classes.

Throughout her life, Gran did most of her party cooking herself, and taught her various cooks the basics of her recipes. So, for example, when she served Chicken Breasts in White Wine for thirty, the cook would brown all those chicken breasts and prepare other essentials such as the salad dressing, but Gran would finish all the dishes as well as make the desserts.

One of her secrets was preparing ahead and keeping many of the preparations and completed dishes in the freezer (see "For the Freezer"). She entertained into her eighties, and in fact had two Valentine's Day parties planned in February of 1988 when she became ill with the heart ailment which would claim her life four years later. I remember well coming into her house on a Saturday or Sunday and finding her making crêpes or preparing her signature pecan or chocolate dessert rolls, all of which could go into the freezer until they were needed for a party.

Over the years, Gran became renowned in Charleston for her entertaining. Her parties, both large and small, included not only her generation but later those of my mother and myself. In May 1988, *Gourmet* magazine featured her food in one of its issues in a spread called "A Charleston Luncheon". The menu, typical of a luncheon she might give, included cheese straws, Charleston shrimp with a rice ring, and "Juliette Staats's Pecan Roll," all photographed in the garden.

Gran thrived on entertaining, whether it was an intimate and simple dinner for six in the dining room, or an elegant, black-tie

Juliette Staats ~ Wedding day, 1927

supper party for thirty in the garden. Even after years of doing so much entertaining, she never lost enthusiasm for planning a menu around old family recipes (and sometimes sprinkling in a few new ones), setting a pretty table (often utilizing her china, linens, silver, and beloved porcelain figurines in groupings as *table garniture*), and most of all enjoying her guests. And somehow she made it all look so easy!

> *That is the very reason I continue to work at this entertaining business. No one ever drops by or has time to visit with each other unless some special occasion is set up. So I shall keep at it as long as able.*
>
> ~ JWS – 11/13/1969

In 1986, the *Today Show* broadcast from Charleston, highlighting among other things the Spoleto Festival, master ironworker Philip Simmons, and the local sweetgrass basket weavers. Gran's interview concluded the show as she related the story of the ghost who is rumored to haunt our house. Shortly after the broadcast, Mollie Fair wrote a letter to the editor which was published in the local newspaper, *The Post and Courier*. Her letter described her reaction to the show, which she said "forced her to acknowledge the passage of time and change, and the need to move forward at any price." She wrote of Gran:

> *She is unquestionably the most wonderful septuagenarian in town. She is low profile, private and exquisite in every way: tall (5'10"), slender, dignified, charming, a personal collector of great breadth and one of the best garden ladies in town.*
>
> *So why did Mrs. Staats being on camera make me cry? I cannot get quite to the bottom of this, but I know it has to do with privacy, integrity and change—hers, mine and Charleston's. I had never realized before how representative she is to me as a woman of character and overwhelming authenticity. When you observe and listen to her from the remove of a TV lens, that authenticity looms large and every facial expression, tilt of the head, sparkle in the eye, intonation of the story has magnified impact.*
>
> *...it is wrenching to see past, present and future pulled together in such dramatic tension. ...She embodied so powerfully in those few moments something so precious of my past, of a city and of a generation of women... .*

Mollie's words say much about why Gran was so special: to her friends, to her family, and indeed to the city of Charleston. She represented a generation of women, an American century, and a gracious lifestyle that we are fast losing in the rapid homogenization of both Charleston and of our larger world.

A Black-Tie Dinner Party in the Garden

CHEESE STRAWS

CHICKEN BREASTS IN WHITE WINE

VEGETABLE SALAD PLATTER WITH
SNAPPY SALAD DRESSING

TOMATO ASPIC WITH HOMEMADE MAYONNAISE

HOT FRENCH BREAD

PECAN ROLL WITH CARAMEL SAUCE

For Gran, the social new year always began in October. By then, she and my grandfather had returned from their annual summer vacation; they were both ready to see old friends and, of course, to enjoy Charleston's famously delicious fall climate. The first party she gave each fall was almost always a black-tie dinner in the garden. Indeed, the garden was her favorite place to entertain; she loved to have luncheons and dinner parties of all sizes there whenever the weather was fair.

Over the years, she was to become especially known for her large, black-tie dinner parties. In the winter, she'd have the living room and adjacent study cleared of furniture so that round tables for six could be scattered throughout; the buffet would be set up in the dining room. In good weather, however, she'd have the tables placed in the largest of her garden rooms. Subtle electric garden lights discreetly lit the pathways, flowerbeds, and parterres. Tall torchères—placed at the terrace's corners and around the lawn's perimeter—illuminated the surrounding oaks and camellias, creating dramatic shadows and conjuring magical effects. All these ingredients—menu, setting, illumination, formal attire—combined to make her black-tie al fresco evenings spectacular.

Graceful sculptures of the four seasons watch over the buffet table in the garden.

For as long as she lived there, my grandmother adored her Charleston house and garden. She and my grandfather purchased the early Georgian structure—built in 1735 and known as the Thomas Rose House—in 1941. It still retains the large, dignified, original panels; unusual arched doorways; robust cornices; and other simple, early Georgian decorations that are nearly as Rose left them. Its masonry exterior—fortified by three-foot-thick brick walls—has survived fires, wars, earthquakes, and hurricanes.

As much as she loved the house, the garden was her special passion. Soon after they purchased the house, Gran commissioned renowned Charleston landscape architect Loutrel Briggs to design the overall garden, which included a pattern garden with elliptical beds—for growing herbs—at the rear of the property. Some years later, she was fortunate to have an opportunity to significantly increase the size of the garden. In 1953—while my grandfather was on safari for six months in Africa—the property to the south of their house came up for sale; my grandmother nervously made the decision on her own to buy it. That property had originally belonged to Thomas Rose. A subsequent owner had subdivided the property and built a house upon it in 1840. My grandparents' original plans included restoring the 1840 house and converting it to a guest house.

Again, Gran called upon Loutrel Briggs, who designed plans for the expanded garden, incorporating the guest house. Interestingly, these plans are still on file at the South Carolina Historical Society today. The portion of the plans which included the guest house, however, was never executed. According to my grandmother, the house was in such deplorable condition that they were forced to demolish it—something I doubt our present-day Board of Architectural Review would allow in the case of an 1840 building.

Instead, Briggs redesigned the expanded space—minus the guest house area—which now includes a large parking court and several separate garden "rooms." When the garden was installed, three feet of rich topsoil was brought in before the planting. Gran was convinced that this topsoil was responsible for the height and health of the live oaks. At first just eight feet tall—the same height as the wall—these trees now tower over the garden and parking area, providing welcome shade during the hot months.

My grandmother loved the fact that a Charleston garden blooms year round. The blooming cycle in her garden begins in the fall with the camellia sasanqua. The camellia japonica—many individual plants now twelve feet tall—begins to bloom in December; throughout January and February, the garden is a sea of its red, pink, white, and variegated blossoms. In March and April, the pink and coral azaleas and lavender wisteria (looking painterly as it climbs the creamy yellow walls of the old stable behind the house) take over. With such beautifully workable elements—privacy, a pleasant design, a garden full of flowers—no wonder Gran took every opportunity to entertain in her garden.

Garden dinner parties usually commenced with cocktails—accompanied by tangy, home-made cheese straws—served in the garden room closest to the house. The buffet was often set up on the "piazza"—Charleston's term for the long veranda which runs the length of the south side of the house. The guests then found their places at the tables, set in the leafy seclusion of the south side of the garden. Here—in an enchanted atmosphere gilded with the flickering light of candles and torchères—they lingered well into the evening.

*C*HEESE *S*TRAWS

Makes about 4 dozen small sticks.

4   tablespoons butter, softened

½   teaspoon salt

½   teaspoon paprika

3   shakes of cayenne pepper

½   pound Cheddar cheese, finely grated

1   cup cake flour (if doubling the recipe, use just 1¾ cups)

Preheat oven to 375°. Cream butter with salt, paprika and cayenne. Add grated cheese and mix thoroughly. Add flour very slowly, and mix until it pulls into a ball. Put dough into a pastry tube or cookie press, and pipe into sticks on an ungreased cookie sheet. If you do not have a pastry tube or cookie press, you may shape the sticks by hand. Bake in the preheated oven for 12 to 14 minutes.

We usually double this recipe, as they go fast. These keep exceptionally well in an airtight tin.

Chicken Breasts in White Wine

Serves 4.

4	tablespoons butter
4	chicken breast halves, boned and skinned
¼	cup flour
¼	pound mushrooms
	Juice of 1 lemon
1	tomato, peeled
1	cup dry white wine
2	tablespoons brandy
1	tablespoon glace de viande
	Dash of cayenne pepper
	Salt to taste
1	tablespoon chopped parsley

Preheat oven to 350°. Melt butter in a large sauté pan. When it has melted and is bubbling, add the chicken breast halves which have been lightly dusted with flour. Let them cook to a golden brown.

Remove the chicken pieces to a casserole dish. Clean the mushrooms and cut them into pieces. Add them to the butter in the pan, and add the lemon juice. Add the tomato, cut into pieces. Stir in the wine, brandy, meat glaze, and seasoning. Pour this sauce mixture over the chicken breasts, and bake about 30 minutes. Remove the chicken to a serving platter. At this point you may if necessary add 2 teaspoons of flour to thicken the sauce slightly. To thicken, add a bit of the sauce to the flour and stir until it is a smooth paste, then stir it gradually into the rest of the sauce. Continue to stir the sauce for 1 to 2 minutes until it is smooth and thickened. Pour the sauce over the chicken and sprinkle with a full tablespoon of chopped parsley.

If you cannot find glace de viande (meat glaze) in your local store, you may substitute ⅓ can beef consommé. You can also purchase or order glace de viande from Williams Sonoma or other specialty stores. This dish can be prepared in advance and refrigerated. If it is cold it should bake 45 minutes. It can easily be multiplied to serve more.

Supper in garden; pastel cloths, hurricane lights with wreaths of corn flowers and daisies. Spotlights. It was a magnificent night–garden was bug free, vigil lights on paths. Everyone enjoyed it.

~ JWS – 6/14/1960

*S*NAPPY *S*ALAD *D*RESSING

Makes about a pint.

1	teaspoon dry mustard
½	teaspoon paprika
1	teaspoon salt
1	tablespoon sugar
¼	teaspoon coarsely ground black pepper
¾	cup olive oil
¼	cup cider vinegar
¼	cup white wine tarragon vinegar
1	tablespoon Worcestershire sauce
2	tablespoons catsup
1	tablespoon finely grated onion (optional)
	Tabasco sauce to taste (optional)
1	clove garlic (optional)

Mix all dry ingredients. Add ¼ cup oil. Mix thoroughly, then add vinegars and remaining ingredients (except garlic). Beat with a fork until well blended. Store in a jar with a cut clove of garlic if desired.

This dressing is a must-have in my refrigerator as well as my mother's and grandmother's. It keeps for months in a jar, and we have a pint or quart jar on hand at all times. When refrigerated, the olive oil will solidify, so before using, let the dressing sit at room temperature.

*V*EGETABLE *S*ALAD *P*LATTER

We serve two salad platters for a buffet luncheon or dinner for 20-30 guests. One platter holds a 4-quart Tomato Aspic ring. This is garnished with lettuce around the edge of the platter, and the ring can be filled with sliced avocado which has been marinated in some of the Snappy Salad Dressing. A bowl of Best Mayonnaise on the side completes the dish. I find many people skip the mayonnaise until they hear it is homemade. Once they taste it, they realize it is totally different from commercial mayonnaise. On the second platter we serve a medley of vegetables, also marinated with Snappy Salad Dressing. This can include baby carrots (either canned or fresh ones which have been boiled and chilled), sliced beets, artichoke hearts marinated in oil and sliced, hearts of palm, cold steamed asparagus spears, and avocado if you are not serving that in the aspic ring. For a warm weather luncheon, you can fill the aspic ring with shrimp salad, made with the homemade mayonnaise and some fresh diced dill, and freshly ground pepper.

**T**OMATO **A**SPIC

7¾	cups (62 ounces) tomato juice
2	stalks celery with leaves
½	yellow onion studded with cloves
½	teaspoon salt
¼	teaspoon finely ground white pepper
1	teaspoon sugar
⅓	cup white wine tarragon vinegar
1½	tablespoons Worcestershire sauce
½	cup catsup
4	envelopes plain unflavored gelatin

In a large pot mix all ingredients except the gelatin. Bring to a simmer and cook for 5 minutes. Strain the tomato juice mixture and measure it exactly. You will need to add 1 envelope of gelatin for every pint of tomato juice. Soften the gelatin in several tablespoons of cold tomato juice, then add it to the hot juice. Stir gently until the gelatin is completely dissolved. Rinse a 2-quart aspic mold or a bowl with cold water. Drain the water, then pour in the hot tomato juice. Let chill several hours or overnight. To unmold, put very hot water into your sink. Carefully set the aspic mold into the sink so that the bottom ½-inch or so is submerged in the hot water. Wiggle it back and forth to loosen the aspic, then invert onto a serving plate. If you leave it too long in the water, it will begin to dissolve. So try it several times quickly, just until it loosens. You can wipe off the edge of the platter around the aspic and garnish the edges with lettuce leaves.

This can easily be doubled. We use a 4-quart mold for a large luncheon or dinner party of 20 to 30 guests.

> *Supper party in the garden—spotlights were perfect, weather perfect with a full moon.*
>
> ~ JWS – 6/20/1959

BEST MAYONNAISE

Makes about 1 pint.

2   eggs or 2 yolks plus 1 whole egg

3-4 tablespoons white wine tarragon vinegar
     (or lemon juice if you prefer)

½   teaspoon salt

½   teaspoon dry mustard or 1 teaspoon Dijon
     mustard

⅛   teaspoon white pepper

1½   cups olive oil

Put eggs, 3 tablespoons vinegar and seasonings into a food processor and blend. With processor running, very slowly add the olive oil in a thin, steady stream. When all the oil has been added, turn off processor and taste. At this point you may add the 4th tablespoon of vinegar if you want a particularly sharp mayonnaise.

PECAN ROLL WITH CARAMEL SAUCE

Serves 12 to 15.

CAKE

6	large eggs at room temperature, separated
¾	cup light brown sugar
1½	cups finely chopped pecans
2	rounded teaspoons cake flour
1	teaspoon baking powder
	Dash of salt
1	teaspoon vanilla
¼	cup sifted powdered sugar

Preheat oven to 375°. Grease a jelly-roll pan, approximately 11x17½ inches. Cover the length with waxed paper, and leave ½-inch or so hanging over the ends. Grease the pan again with the waxed paper in it, and flour lightly. Separate the eggs and beat the yolks with the brown sugar. Mix in the flour and baking powder, and add the finely chopped pecans and the vanilla. It is best to chop the pecans by hand. If you do use a food processor, process in very small batches and make sure the nuts are chopped fine without over-processing to the point the nuts become oily. Add the salt to the egg whites and beat until stiff but not dry. Fold the egg whites into the nut mixture. Spread the mixture evenly in the prepared pan, and bake 18-20 minutes. While the cake is baking, take a clean tea towel and cover it with waxed paper. Dust the paper with powdered sugar. When the cake is done, immediately turn it out onto the fresh waxed paper. Carefully peel off the waxed paper that lined the baking pan. Trim off (about ¼-inch) the strip along the sides of the cake which has turned somewhat crispy during baking. This will prevent the cake from splitting when rolled. While the cake is still warm, dust it lightly with powdered sugar and roll up lengthwise inside the waxed paper and towel. This can all be done the day ahead and refrigerated.

FILLING

1	cup heavy cream, whipped
2	tablespoons powdered sugar
½	teaspoon vanilla

Whip cream until stiff and mix in powdered sugar and vanilla. When ready to serve, gently unroll cake and spread with the whipped cream mixture. Roll up like a jelly-roll and put on a platter. Cut into slices about ½-inch and serve with Caramel Sauce.

You may use the brown sugar sauce or the true caramelized sugar sauce below.

BROWN SUGAR CARAMEL SAUCE

2	cups light brown sugar
	Pinch salt
½	cup water
4	tablespoons butter or ½ cup heavy cream
1	teaspoon vanilla

Mix the brown sugar, salt, and water and cook slowly, stirring constantly, until the sugar is dissolved. Bring to a good boil, then add the butter or cream and the vanilla. Serve the sauce warm, but not hot.

CARAMEL SAUCE

1	cup sugar
½	cup water
⅓	cup heavy cream

Mix the sugar and water in a heavy pan, and cook without stirring until the sugar dissolves, brushing the crystals off the side of the pan with a pastry brush dipped in water. Let this come to a boil, then turn the heat down slightly and continue cooking without stirring. It will bubble on the surface and eventually turn a golden brown as the sugar caramelizes. Remove from the heat and stir in the heavy cream. Be careful, as the hot caramelized sugar will spatter when the cream is added.

This roll can be made a day ahead. Sprinkle the unfilled roll while warm in powdered sugar, roll in waxed paper and a clean tea towel or foil, and refrigerate overnight. Let it warm slightly to room temperature, unroll gently and fill with cream. The filled roll can also be frozen whole. Take it out to thaw at room temperature for about 1½ hours before serving.

A Soufflé Supper

CHEESE SOUFFLÉ

GREEN SALAD WITH SNAPPY DRESSING

ETHEL'S HOT BISCUIT

HOMEMADE JAMS

For many years in Charleston my grandmother had the dearest evening cook, Ethel Williams. Ethel, a tiny lady not five feet tall, was truly a delight. She came every week day at four-thirty. The first thing she would do each evening was close the big double gates into the garden. In those days, the unwritten rule in Charleston was that if a garden gate was open, you were welcome to enter. Gran always followed that gracious local custom. During the daytime, she welcomed anyone to wander in and visit the garden. As was the hospitable habit of many Charlestonians of that era, she loved to engage visitors and passersby in conversation.

After closing the gates, Ethel would begin to get ready for tea. Tea time was a tradition my grandparents had adopted following a trip to England. For as long as I can remember and wherever we were—whether in Charleston or the mountains of North Carolina—we had tea with them in the late afternoon. Gran loved to include guests at tea, so the daily ritual also often provided an opportunity to catch up with friends or visitors in a warm, congenial setting.

One of the things I especially cherish is that my own children got to enjoy tea time with "Gran-Gran." In their early years—when we were living across the street from Gran—we usually followed nap time with a stroll to the park a few blocks away. On our way home we would stop by for tea. Gran loved having her "treasures" at the tea table. I can tell you that there were many afternoons at that stage that my two wild young children didn't seem very much like treasures to me! Ethel would bring the tea tray; each child had a child-sized chair to sit in. The tray would be set with our teacups along with a special demitasse

The original kitchen with its old brick ovens makes a cozy nook for this intimate supper. The table is set with eighteenth century Chinese exportware.

cup for each child; Ethel always made sure my young daughter got the rosebud cup. While I believe that much of their early tea consumption consisted of inordinate quantities of sugar and milk, it was a special time for all the generations to share. And, to this day, I know that if my children are plunked down anywhere in the world, they remember the proper tea etiquette.

After tea was over, Ethel would begin getting ready for supper. Gran always maintained the southern tradition of having the big meal at midday; if she were dining alone, supper might well be a cup of soup and a navel orange in season. But one of our favorite suppers—just for family or a few guests—was cheese soufflé. It was always served with Ethel's delicious hot biscuit (we never called them "biscuits"), several varieties of homemade jam that had been made in the summer, and a fresh green salad with Snappy Dressing.

Gran loved to offer us seconds on the cheese soufflé; rich as it was, she insisted, "It's just egg white, darling." But thankfully, in acknowledgement of the richness of the soufflé and the sweetness of the jam, she always added, "Remember, there's no dessert." Another memorable observation came from my husband who always said "soufflé waits for no man"—a good rule to follow as the soufflé should be served promptly before it starts to fall. We especially love to make this soufflé with the same cheese that Gran used, a sharp Cheddar available from Sugarbush Farms in Woodstock, Vermont. We keep on hand the three-pound wheel in its black wax coating, and I promise you there's no Cheddar like it!

Cathy and the two treasures came for tea the day after I got back.

~ JWS – 1/15/1987

I will warn you too about Ethel's biscuit: they are not the big, flaky, southern biscuits you may expect. Instead, they are thin and very short, made with lots of vegetable shortening. In addition to being delicious with homemade preserves either for supper as in this menu, or for breakfast, they make perfect ham biscuits. Just add a sliver of salty Virginia smoked ham and, if you wish, a little mustard inside the split biscuit.

I am grateful to my brother Phil who, on one of his last visits to Charleston before Ethel retired, followed her to the kitchen on soufflé night and asked if he could watch her make her biscuits and write everything down. Ethel added and mixed ingredients by feel rather than by measuring; without Phil's foresight in recording the measurements, I would never have been able to recreate them. The first time I made these biscuits, my southern husband proclaimed them "hockey pucks." But after a few more batches I finally got them right. I might add that the biscuits seem to turn out best for me when I use the same old bowl and pastry blender that Ethel did; her hand is so much in this menu—and these pages. We now enjoy her best-of-all biscuits with or without cheese soufflé.

Catherine Staats Forrester and her Gran-Gran, 1987

*C*HEESE *S*OUFFLÉ

Serves 4. Can be doubled to serve 6 to 8.

4   tablespoons butter
4   tablespoons flour
1½   cups whole milk, scalded
½   teaspoon salt
     Dash cayenne pepper
½   pound good quality Cheddar cheese, grated
2   teaspoons onion juice (optional)
6   eggs at room temperature, separated

Preheat the oven to 300° (or 325° if you prefer a moister center to the soufflé). Melt the butter in the top of a double boiler. Add flour, salt and cayenne and stir until well mixed. Gradually add the hot milk and continue stirring as it cooks until it is thick and smooth. Remove from the heat and add the grated cheese. Stir until well blended, then add the 6 egg yolks, which have been slightly beaten. Cool mixture until it is room temperature. Beat the 6 egg whites until stiff, but not dry. Fold them into the egg yolk/cheese mixture. Pour into a 2-quart soufflé dish, and bake 1 hour and 15 minutes at 300°. You may also bake it at 325° for 1 hour, which yields a soufflé which is a bit more moist in the middle.

Variation: For a more savory cheese soufflé, add ¾ teaspoon hot powdered mustard and ½ teaspoon curry powder.

*E*THEL'S *H*OT *B*ISCUIT

Makes about 2 dozen thin 2-inch biscuits.

2   cups sifted flour (do not use one of the traditional southern biscuit flours for these biscuits; they are not meant to be fluffy)
3   teaspoons baking powder
½   teaspoon salt
½   cup plus 1 tablespoon vegetable shortening
⅓   cup whole milk (you may need an extra tablespoon or so)

Preheat the oven to 425°. Sift the dry ingredients. Using a pastry blender, cut in the shortening until it is the consistency of coarse cornmeal. Add the milk to form a soft dough, but not sticky. If the dough seems too dry, you may need to add an extra tablespoon or so of milk. Roll the dough out to a thickness of about ¼-inch. Cut into rounds, and bake at 425° for 12 minutes until lightly browned. Serve while hot.

Chapter V
November

Thanksgiving Dinner

Old Dutch Rum Punch

Roast Turkey with Rice Stuffing

Whole Cranberry Sauce

Great-Grandmother's Escalloped Oysters

Steamed Green Beans

Candied Sweet Potatoes

Pumpkin Pie

Pecan Pie

*T*hanksgiving is my favorite holiday. The weather is usually clear and brisk—cool enough for a fire—although I remember several balmy years when we had Thanksgiving dinner in the garden. With the young people home from school and the men and boys often hunting for much of the weekend, the city resumes its old, languorous pace. Thanksgiving is also the holiday at which our family serves all the familiar recipes; each year they are like old friends we haven't seen in a long time. (Of course, there's nothing to prevent us from making these recipes at other times of the year, but we rarely do!)

We always have a fresh roast turkey with stewed whole cranberries; I also make my great-grandmother's Escalloped Oysters, full of fat, briny local oysters. The stuffing in this menu is made with rice, as befits the Lowcountry, whose fortune was made through the great rice plantations. As Sam Stoney writes in *Charleston: Azaleas and Old Bricks,* "I must be most serious with you when I ask you to realize that rice in Charleston is more an institution than a cereal, and warn you that until you subscribe to that belief, you will never altogether understand the history of the town."

The colors in the late-nineteenth century Foley China echo the palette of the dining room, and make for a festive Thanksgiving table.

We end with Gran's Pumpkin Pie, which is really a pumpkin chiffon pie. Over the years I've entertained a number of people who swore they didn't like pumpkin pie, but loved this version. Two things make it so different and so good: first, using a large quantity of spices (cinnamon, cloves, ginger, and nutmeg); and second, beating the egg whites separately (which gives it a much lighter texture than most pumpkin pies).

I also always make a second pie, Gran's Pecan Pie, which again is different from most. Instead of the light brown sugar and light corn syrup used in the majority of recipes, this one calls for the dark varieties of each, making it intensely flavored and very rich. It is also filled with good southern pecans. Years ago, when I was visiting my cousin, Tony, and his wife in Istanbul, he asked if I knew how to make my mother's pecan pie, which he loved. After they left to drive to Ankara, a full day's trip, I took to the kitchen to see what I could concoct, not having a clue what the family recipe called for. Since there was nothing in the house but dark brown sugar and dark corn syrup, that's what I used, only to find out later that this variation on ingredients is exactly what makes the recipe so special. Maybe that's how it was invented all those generations ago!

In Charleston, the tradition of the midday dinner prevails; most families have their Thanksgiving dinner then, as well. This allows time for clean up, followed by a leisurely stroll around the city—a definite plus for digestion! We follow the family tradition of setting a formal table in the dining room. Just as in Gran's day, the soft green of the walls and coral accents in the niches and needlepoint rug set the tone for the table. We often use the pale peach damask cloth with matching napkins, handed down from my great-grandmother. The porcelain might be an antique pattern in hues of peach or green, or the more contemporary—but traditional—"Sacred Butterfly," a white and coral pattern reproduced by Mottahedah for Historic Charleston Foundation.

Today Virginia picked 5 pounds of Charleston shrimp and I put them in the freezer. I will get another 5 pounds soon, as the shrimp season is almost finished, and I think everyone should have a shrimp supper when they are here. These are not like the frozen shrimp one buys. Oysters are coming in now, and I am thinking of my son-in-law. They should be plentiful at Christmas, but I shall speak ahead just in case.

~ JWS – 11/3/76

OLD DUTCH RUM PUNCH

1   quart Jamaican dark rum
1   pint brandy
     Juice of 3 large oranges
     Juice of 3 lemons
     Cinnamon bark
     Whole cloves
     Sugar to taste
2   tablespoons butter
½   teaspoon Angostura bitters
2   tablespoons Grenadine

Preheat a large punch bowl, and pour in the rum and brandy. In a medium saucepan, bring the orange juice, lemon juice, spices, and sugar to the boiling point with 1½ quarts hot water. Stir in the butter until it is melted. Add to rum and brandy in the punch bowl. Stir in the bitters and Grenadine, and serve immediately.

RICE STUFFING

This will be enough stuffing for a 10- to 12-pound turkey.

3   cups cooked rice
1   egg
2   tablespoons whole milk
1   small onion, finely chopped
1½   cups chopped celery
2   tablespoons butter, melted
½   cup chopped parsley
2   teaspoons salt
2   teaspoons mixed dried herbs
¼   teaspoon mace
2   tablespoons Worcestershire sauce

Cook rice as you usually do, and have it dry and fluffy. Beat the egg lightly and mix with the milk. Stir the onion, celery, butter, and seasonings into the rice, add the milk and egg mixture and stir all together well.

> *I am anxious to do some holiday cooking, and I have ordered my Virginia hams already.*
>
> ~ JWS – 10/19/1976

Whole Cranberry Sauce

About 1 quart.

1½-2 cups sugar

2 cups water

4 cups fresh cranberries (about 1 pound)

Boil sugar and water together for 5 minutes. Add cranberries and boil without stirring until the skins pop, about 5 minutes. Remove from the heat and let cool in pan undisturbed.

This keeps in jars in the refrigerator for months.

Great Grandmother's Escalloped Oysters

Serves 6.

2 pints oysters

10 ounces oyster crackers

¼ pound butter

½-¾ cup cream (you may use half & half or heavier cream)

Salt and pepper to taste

Preheat the oven to 350°. For this dish you may use a soufflé dish or similar casserole, which gives a crispy top and moist interior, or use a larger shallow casserole which gives more crispiness throughout. Grease the dish with butter. Crush the crackers until they are uniformly fine. Put in the casserole ⅓ of the crushed crackers. Cover with a layer of half of the oysters, and dot heavily with butter, then sprinkle with salt and pepper. Repeat the layers, ending with the crackers. Pour some of the oyster liqueur over the dish, then pour medium-thick cream over all. The cream should come almost to the top of the dish, but not over the crackers. Bake for 45 minutes at 350°, until the dish is bubbling and brown on the top.

This can easily be multiplied.

Candied Sweet Potatoes

2   pounds sweet potatoes (about 3 large)

1   cup light brown sugar

4   tablespoons butter

¼   cup water

¼   teaspoon cinnamon

     Pinch nutmeg

Preheat oven to 350°. Boil the potatoes in their jackets for about 20 minutes until slightly tender. Meanwhile, in a saucepan, make a syrup of the brown sugar, butter, water, cinnamon and nutmeg and bring it to a boil. Let the potatoes cool, peel them and slice into ½-inch slices. Arrange the slices in a shallow baking pan and pour the syrup over the top. Bake for 1 hour, spooning the syrup over the top from time to time until the potatoes are candied.

There are two types of sweet potatoes—one with thin yellow skin and pale yellow flesh, and the other with a darker, thicker skin and orange flesh. These are frequently called yams, although they are not true yams. The orange-fleshed sweet potato is moister and sweeter and should be used here. This dish can be done ahead until the potatoes are turned into the baking pan, and then finished in the oven.

Pumpkin Pie

2   eggs at room temperature

2   cups canned stewed pumpkin

2   tablespoons butter, melted

1   cup cream

1   cup sugar

1   teaspoon salt

⅛   teaspoon nutmeg

¼   teaspoon ginger

½   teaspoon powdered cloves

2   teaspoons cinnamon

Prepare a pie crust, and line a 10-inch pie pan. Preheat the oven to 350°. Separate the eggs and beat the yolks slightly. In a large mixing bowl, combine the pumpkin, melted butter, cream, egg yolks, sugar, and spices and mix well. Beat the egg whites until stiff, but not dry, and fold into the pumpkin mixture. Pour into prepared crust and bake at 350° for 60 to 65 minutes, or until a knife inserted into the center comes out clean. Cool and serve at room temperature.

This can also be prepared ahead and frozen before baking. To bake a frozen pie, remove from the freezer 10 minutes before baking. Bake for 10 minutes at 400°, then lower heat to 300° and bake for 1½ hours longer. The pie is done when a knife inserted in the center comes out clean.

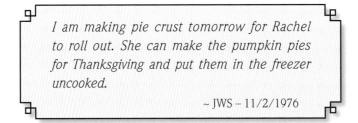

I am making pie crust tomorrow for Rachel to roll out. She can make the pumpkin pies for Thanksgiving and put them in the freezer uncooked.

~ JWS – 11/2/1976

Pecan Pie

½   cup butter, softened

1   cup dark brown sugar

3   eggs

1   cup dark corn syrup

1-1 ½ cups pecans, chopped very coarsely

1   teaspoon vanilla

     Dash of salt

Line a 9-inch pie pan with a crust. Cream the butter and sugar until the mixture is light and fluffy. Add the eggs which have been beaten slightly, and the corn syrup. Stir in the chopped pecans. The recipe calls for 1 cup, but you may add an extra ¼ to ½ cup if you like it nuttier. If you add a full 1 ½ cups pecans, you will need a 10-inch pie pan. Stir in the vanilla and salt, mixing well. Pour the mixture into the prepared crust, and bake at 400° for 10 minutes. Turn the heat down to 350°, and bake for 45 minutes more. Cool and serve at room temperature.

This also makes 12 individual tarts.

A Black-Tie Debutante Dinner Party

OYSTERS ON THE HALF SHELL WITH VINAIGRETTE

CHICKEN BREASTS IN SAUCE SUPREME

RICE WITH RAISINS AND CURRANTS

SPINACH RING

CHOCOLATE ROLL WITH CHOCOLATE SAUCE

*W*hen a child is born in Charleston, one of the first things the mother must do is find a partner for dancing school. Sometimes these arrangements are even tentatively made before birth. But in any case, each girl who signs up for dancing school must do so with a partner to ensure that each class has an equal number of girls and boys. For decades, the school was taught on Wednesday afternoons by Emily Fishburne Whaley, who started it in about 1945. Since 1978, it has been carried on by her daughter, Emily Whaley Whipple.

Beginning in fourth grade, the children attend once a week for four years; each spring the year concludes with a cotillion at which the children demonstrate for their parents what they have learned during the year. The boys must wear coat-and-tie; the girls wear demure dresses and white cotton gloves. For the girls, the beginning of dancing school is very exciting, and even in fourth grade there is much to-do each week in choosing a dress and styling hair. For the boys, there is, predictably, less excitement. When we asked my son after his first day of dancing school which girls he had danced with, he replied, "I don't know. I didn't look."

Many years after completing dancing school, the young people have a chance to dust off all those waltz and foxtrot steps and put them to practical use during the debutante season. For generations, young ladies made their debut after their first year at college. In the late 1990s, however, Charleston parents—concerned about underage drinking—got together and decided to delay the debutante season until the young people had reached the age of twenty-one. For a debutante now, the season begins the summer before her senior year in college and continues throughout the year, with the biggest parties being held at Thanksgiving and Christmas. The most famous, of course, is the St. Cecilia Ball, held

Coalport dessert plates and antique silver wine coolers lend formality to the setting for the debutante and her guests.

in January, but one must be a long-time Charlestonian to be a member of the St. Cecelia Society. The Society was founded in 1737 to give concerts, and has held its annual ball since 1822. Membership is passed through the male line in the family, and revoked in the case of divorce. No alcohol except sherry is served at the St. Cecelia, but pre-ball cocktail parties allow guests to arrive in high spirits.

I remember my grandmother's tales about earlier decades when some Charlestonians closed the shutters on their houses on the evening of the third Thursday in January, so that others would not know they were at home—and not attending the ball. Over the years, however, other debutante societies have been established for those who do not have membership in the St. Cecelia: the Carolina Assembly, which holds its ball in November, and the Charleston Cotillion, which holds its in December.

At the balls, parents, grandparents, and guests of their generation generally arrive at eight o'clock. Shortly afterward, the debutantes are formally presented to the assembly. By nine o'clock or so the young people begin to arrive and the older generations fade away. Many of the young people have left Charleston for boarding schools after their first eight years of schooling, and from there gone on to college. The debutante season, therefore, occurring as it does over the holidays, gives them the opportunity to renew old acquaintances—and frequently to party till dawn.

Throughout the debutante season are scattered other, smaller affairs: a ladies' tea, a small dance in honor of one or two debutantes, or perhaps a lovely reception at home. Gran loved to host debutante suppers in honor of the daughters or granddaughters of close friends. These elegant, black-tie parties for thirty were truly special for "the young." And, many years later, I still hear people mention Gran's parties with fondness. As one former debutante recently said to me, "I still remember the menu your grandmother served. At that young age, I didn't appreciate the effort it took. How generous she was to go to all that trouble on my behalf."

> *I have all of the information now on debutantes and parties for the boys' schedule. I may send Phil and Jim a list of potential guests for their supper party. One or two at least of this year's debutantes they will have to have, willy nilly. But I want the majority of boys and girls to be the ones they especially want.*
>
> ~ JWS – 10/19/76

OYSTERS ON THE HALF SHELL WITH VINAIGRETTE

Even young people in Charleston have a taste for fresh local oysters. These are served with a piquant vinaigrette.

18	fresh, raw oysters, opened and left on shell
½	cup white wine tarragon vinegar
1	tablespoon finely minced shallot
2	dozen peppercorns, chopped coarsely
1	teaspoon finely minced parsley
1	tablespoon whole mustard seed
½	teaspoon salt

Open the oysters and leave them in their shells, arranged on plates as desired. Mix all the other ingredients together, and blend well. Dress each oyster with about ½ tablespoon of the dressing, or to taste.

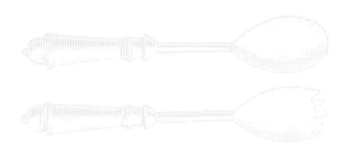

Chicken Breasts in Sauce Supreme

Makes 2 quarts.

This is a perfect dish for a large luncheon or buffet supper.

Sauce Supreme

½	pound mushrooms
½	pound (2 sticks) plus 1 tablespoon butter
2	teaspoons lemon juice
1	cup flour
6	cups chicken broth
2	cups sour cream
1	teaspoon salt
½	teaspoon ground white pepper
1	tablespoon Worcestershire sauce
2	teaspoons catsup

Clean mushrooms with a damp paper towel and cut into chunks. Melt the 1 tablespoon butter in a sauté pan and add mushroom pieces. Add lemon juice and cook, stirring for several minutes until the mushrooms are softened and the liquid has been released. Set aside. In large saucepan, melt the remaining ½ pound butter and add the flour. Stir until thick and smooth (about 3 minutes), but do not let it brown. Gradually add the chicken broth, about ½ to 1 cup at a time, stirring well after each addition, and let it come to a boil. Stir constantly until it is thick and smooth, about 10 minutes. If you have lumps, whisk it briefly. Remove ½ cup of this and mix it with the sour cream. Remove sauce from heat and add sour cream mixture, mixing well. Do not let sauce boil after the sour cream is added. Season with salt, pepper, Worcestershire sauce, and catsup, then stir in the mushrooms and mushroom broth. At this point, the sauce can be frozen until ready to use.

FINISHING THE CHICKEN

Serves 8 to 12.

¾ pound mushrooms

½ pound butter (2 sticks)

1½ tablespoons lemon juice

1 quart sauce supreme

½ cup sour cream

½ cup dry white wine

12 half breasts of chicken, skinned and boned

Preheat oven to 350°. Clean and slice mushrooms. Melt 2 tablespoons of the butter in a large sauté pan, and add mushrooms and lemon juice. Cook, stirring for several minutes until the mushrooms are softened and the liquid has been released. You will need about ½ cup of mushroom broth. Warm the sauce supreme in a double boiler or non-reactive sauce pan. Add the mushroom broth, sour cream, and white wine. Reserve the mushrooms. In a large sauté pan, melt 1 stick butter. Brown the chicken breasts in the butter and remove them to a shallow oven proof casserole. Scatter the cooked mushrooms on top of the chicken breasts. Pour the sauce over the chicken breasts and mushrooms, and finish cooking in a 350° oven for 1 hour.

For a large party use 2 quarts Sauce Supreme and 40 chicken breast halves. Finish in oven for 1½ hours. You can make the sauce well ahead and freeze. Chicken breasts can be browned the day ahead, and sauce added when you finish cooking.

RICE WITH RAISINS AND CURRANTS

Serves 8.

This is also called pilaf, or purlow in the Lowcountry, and is somewhat similar to a risotto in that the rice is first stirred into melted butter, and then the hot stock is added. The addition of raisins and currants makes it unique.

4	tablespoons butter
2	tablespoons finely grated onion
2	cups rice
¾	teaspoon salt
⅓	cup golden raisins
⅙	cup currants
3	cups chicken broth

Preheat the oven to 350°. In a deep saucepan, melt the butter. Add grated onion, and cook gently for a few minutes until translucent. Add the rice and stir it around in the butter mixture, then add the salt, raisins and currants. In a separate saucepan, bring the broth to the boil, and pour it over the rice mixture, stirring well. Put the mixture into a casserole and bake covered for 45 minutes. Fluff the rice before serving.

This is wonderful for a large dinner party. It can be prepared ahead of time and put in the oven before serving. For a party for 30, the amounts are as follows:

½	pound butter
½	cup grated onion
8	cups rice
1	tablespoon salt
2	cups mixed raisins and currants
12	cups chicken broth

Bake for 1½ hours.

Spinach Ring

Serves 8.

This is one of a number of recipes of my grandmother's that appeared in Charleston Receipts, the original cookbook of the Junior League of Charleston.

1 ½ cups cooked, chopped spinach

2 tablespoons butter

2 tablespoons flour

½ cup milk, scalded

3 eggs, separated

½ teaspoon salt

¼ teaspoon pepper

1 tablespoon finely grated onion

Preheat oven to 350°. Cook spinach, drain well and chop. Grease a 2-quart ring mold, and set aside. Melt butter over low heat. Add flour, and stir until it is smooth. Slowly add hot milk, stirring with a wooden spoon or a whisk, and cook until it becomes thick. Stir the egg yolks into the butter mixture, mixing well. Add salt and pepper. Stir in the chopped spinach and the grated onion, then cool. Beat the egg whites until stiff but not dry, and fold them into the spinach mixture. Turn into the greased mold, set the mold into a shallow pan of water, and bake about 30 minutes. Turn out carefully onto a platter.

This ring can be filled with creamed eggs, mushrooms, or carrots.

CHOCOLATE ROLL WITH CHOCOLATE SAUCE

This is the chocolate version of Gran's signature Pecan Roll in the menu for the Black-Tie Dinner in the Garden.

CAKE

2	ounces unsweetened chocolate
6	eggs, separated
⅔	cup powdered sugar
½	teaspoon vanilla
2	teaspoons cake flour
¼	teaspoon salt
½	teaspoon baking soda
1	teaspoon baking powder

Preheat oven to 325°. Grease a jelly-roll pan, approximately 8x15 inches. Cover the length with waxed paper, and leave ½-inch or so hanging over the ends. Grease the pan again with the waxed paper in it, and flour lightly. Melt the chocolate in a double boiler, or a bowl set over hot water. In the large bowl of an electric mixer, beat the egg yolks until thick and lemon colored. Sift the powdered sugar, and add gradually to the egg yolks, continuing to beat until well blended. Stir in the melted chocolate and the vanilla. Sift the cake flour with the salt, baking soda, and baking powder, and add to the egg yolk mixture. Beat the egg whites until they form stiff peaks, and fold into the batter. Spread batter evenly in prepared pan. Bake at 325° for 18 minutes. While the cake is baking, take a clean tea towel and cover it with waxed paper. Dust the paper with powdered sugar. When the cake is done, immediately turn it out onto the fresh waxed paper. Carefully peel off the paper that lined the baking pan. Trim off (about ¼-inch) the strip along the sides of the cake which has turned somewhat crispy during baking. This will prevent the cake from splitting when rolled. While the cake is still warm, dust it lightly with powdered sugar and roll up lengthwise inside the waxed paper and towel. This can all be done the day ahead and refrigerated.

FILLING

1	cup heavy cream, whipped	
2	tablespoons powdered sugar	
½	teaspoon vanilla	

Whip cream stiff and add powdered sugar and vanilla. When ready to serve, unroll cake gently and spread with whipped cream filling. Roll up like a jelly roll and put on a platter. Cut into slices about ½-inch and serve with Chocolate Sauce.

Flavored whipped cream — if you like the combination of mint and chocolate, you may omit the vanilla above, and add to the whipped cream 3 tablespoons crushed candy canes. For coffee-flavored whipped cream — add 2 teaspoons instant coffee to the cream, and stir until the coffee crystals are completely dissolved and mixed in.

CHOCOLATE SAUCE

⅓	cup water
2	ounces unsweetened chocolate
1	tablespoon butter
1	cup sugar
2	tablespoons light corn syrup
1	teaspoon vanilla or dark rum

Boil the water. Melt the chocolate in a double boiler. In a heavy medium-sized saucepan, melt the butter and combine with the melted chocolate, blending well. Add the boiling water. Stir well and add the sugar and corn syrup. Allow the sauce to boil for 5 minutes, and do not stir. Let cool and stir in vanilla or rum.

If you want a sauce that hardens (for example over ice cream), let it boil 8 minutes.

Christmas Dinner

CHAMPAGNE COCKTAIL À LA BAUMANIÈRE

OYSTER STEW

ROAST GOOSE WITH APPLE AND RAISIN STUFFING

DANISH RED CABBAGE

WILD RICE AND MUSHROOM CASSEROLE

PLUM PUDDING WITH HARD SAUCE

Christmas in Charleston, like everywhere, has become more commercialized, especially since the late 1980s when Charleston Place hotel was built. The new hotel sparked the re-vitalization of King Street and the downtown shopping district; in the past twenty years, Charleston has metamorphosed into something of a shopping mecca. But the traditions of Christmas still abound, as evidenced by the holiday lights strung in the public parks; special services, performances, and pageants held at local churches and schools; and many festive parties given throughout the season.

When I was first married, we always went to the midnight service at St. Michael's Episcopal Church. At the ringing of the bells, we walked the few blocks through the night to join friends for the service. Afterward, we might stop by a neighbor's house to enjoy Christmas cheer—usually frosty frozen Brandy Alexanders—with mutual friends from a mix of generations. Finally, after midnight, we'd stroll home through the quiet, starry darkness. When our children were born, we attended the children's service with its traditional Christmas pageant before coming home for our Christmas Eve supper. After the children were in bed, the adults would gather in the formal drawing room—where the tall, fragrant fir tree glowed in the window—and sip eggnog while assembling toys and placing gifts under the tree.

In my younger years we lived in Ohio, where my early lessons about cooking came to a great extent from our neighbor, Matina Thomas. Aunt Tina was an accomplished cook. I remember so many times going to her house and sitting on a stool at the small island in her kitchen while Aunt Tina removed trays of baklava (redolent of honey and cinnamon) from the oven, or loaves of yeasty, aromatic bread. For almost thirty years after we moved from Ohio to California, Aunt Tina sent two loaves of her special Greek

Late nineteenth century Spode plates are combined with Limoges rimmed soup plates in front of the drawing room fire. Champagne cocktails served in balloon glasses from l'Oustau de Baumanière are a celebratory start to the Christmas holiday.

Christmas bread to us every year; it was always the centerpiece of our Christmas Eve supper. Several years ago she passed the recipe on to me, and now I make it for our family and send a loaf to her as well.

The yeasty, slightly sweet loaf is washed in egg and sprinkled with sesame seeds. We always serve it with homemade soup—often turkey soup made from the leftover Thanksgiving turkey. The turkey can be frozen after Thanksgiving until it's time to make the soup; the soup itself freezes well in small containers that last throughout the year. With it we serve a simple green salad. The meal concludes with Pecan Tea Cakes and Tante's Shortbread for dessert—both must-haves at the holiday season (see index).

Christmas Eve was never complete without filling the stockings to overflowing (always stuffing an orange in the toe) and hanging them by the fireplace. Continuing a tradition my parents had started when my brothers and I were young, "Santa" always hung a filled stocking on the doorknob of each child's door after the last little one had fallen asleep. The children would invariably wake around four in the morning and entertain themselves excitedly with everything Santa had brought. Then they'd fall back to sleep until eight o'clock or so, when it was time for Christmas breakfast.

One of the real delights at Christmastime—wherever you live—is enjoying the lights and decorations around the community. Few houses in historic Charleston are covered with the usual strings of lights one sees in other parts of the country. Rather, Charlestonians seem to decorate more subtly: by placing a traditional wreath of evergreen or magnolia leaves (often garnished with holly or popcorn berries) on the front door, or by positioning a lighted tree in a front hall or window, where it can be enjoyed by passersby. We most often buy a Frasier fir grown at one of the many Christmas tree farms in North Carolina, and place it in the center window of the upstairs drawing room. Since the ceiling is twelve feet high, getting the requisite eleven-foot tree up and down

the staircase is a perennial logistical challenge. But it is always worthwhile, for the tree—with its sparkling white lights—is at its most exquisite when viewed from the darkened street below.

For many years, family friends hosted a wonderful Christmas Day tradition. After the Christmas breakfast had been cleaned up, the wrapping paper thrown away, and the dinner put in the oven, we would walk to their house for a Christmas Day drop-in. Families—many like ours with four generations—would come to enjoy a glass of Christmas cheer in the late morning before going back home for Christmas dinner. Gran often said that one of the things she especially loved about Charleston was that all the generations mingled together, and I think this Christmas Day celebration is the best example of that. Besides, we were always amazed that they could have their house tidy enough to welcome guests in the middle of Christmas Day!

> ...by the time one has reached the half-century mark, a Charlestonian is likely to have known five generations of any family.
>
> ~ ELIZABETH O'NEILL VERNER
> *MELLOWED BY TIME*, 1941

Christmas dinner for us was set formally in the dining room with my great-grandmother's damask or lace linens, and the formal Spode porcelain with its red-and-gold border. We might begin with balloon glasses filled with Champagne Cocktail à la Baumanière, which we had discovered during a stay at the famous Oustau de Baumanière in Les Baux, Provence, in the seventies. Gran and I experimented with the ingredients until we approximated the original—a citrus-y champagne and orange combination—which in our version includes both triple sec and orange curaçao.

CHAMPAGNE COCKTAIL À LA BAUMANIÈRE

4 cocktails.

1   bottle dry champagne
1½ teaspoons orange curaçao
2   tablespoons cognac
2   tablespoons sweet vermouth
2   tablespoons Grand Marnier
    Angostura bitters
4   sugar cubes

Add liqueurs to champagne and stir slightly. Into each of 4 large wine glasses put one sugar cube with 2 drops of Angostura bitters. Crush sugar slightly. Pour the champagne mixture over the sugar cube and garnish with an orange slice and a strawberry.

> Today we are finally cooking plum puddings for next year. I had used them all, thought I would not make any more. But every single one of the young in both Wiles families especially mentioned the plum puddings, so I melted. I have been ten days getting beef suet that was fit for use. This was the third batch, and fortunately I was able to make three times the recipe.
>
> ~ JWS – 1/31/73

OYSTER STEW

Serves 4.

2   pints fresh oysters, with liquid
    Dash cayenne pepper
    Pinch salt
    Generous pinch celery salt
2   cups whole milk
1   cup heavy cream
1   tablespoon butter
    Paprika

Put oysters in a saucepan with at least ¼ cup oyster liquid. Add cayenne, salt, and celery salt. Bring to a quick boil. Boil for one minute, skim foam off the top, and add the milk and cream. Just as it reaches the boiling point, add the butter. Ladle into bowls and sprinkle with paprika.

ROAST GOOSE

Serves 6 to 8.

6	pound goose
	Salt
2	slices bacon
1	onion, chopped
1	cup dry white wine
1	tablespoon butter
½	teaspoon paprika
½	teaspoon freshly ground black pepper

Preheat oven to 375°. Clean goose, and rub the cavity with salt. Stuff the cavity with Apple and Raisin Stuffing and fasten with skewers. Stuff the neck, pulling down the skin under the bird, and secure with a skewer. Place the bacon in the bottom of a heavy casserole or roasting pan. Add the onion, wine and butter. Place the goose on top, and sprinkle with salt, pepper and paprika. Roast, covered for 1 hour 15 minutes. Remove the cover, turn up the oven to 400°, and continue roasting, basting occasionally, until the goose has browned nicely or until the juice runs clear when pierced with a fork. This takes about 20 minutes longer.

APPLE AND RAISIN STUFFING

Enough for a 10-pound goose or turkey.

½	cup diced salt pork
1	cup chopped celery
1	cup chopped onion
½	cup chopped parsley
6	medium-sized tart apples, peeled and diced
¼-½	cup sugar
7	cups soft bread crumbs
1	cup raisins
2	teaspoons salt

Fry salt pork until crisp. Remove and reserve pieces. Cook celery, onion and parsley in the fat for 3 minutes; then remove and reserve. Put apples in fat, sprinkle with sugar (the amount depends on the tartness of the apples, and your own preference). Cover and cook slowly until tender. Uncover and cook until slightly glazed. Add bread crumbs, raisins, and reserved salt pork, celery, onion, parsley and salt. Cool slightly and stuff goose or turkey.

Try substituting dried cranberries for the raisins.

Danish Red Cabbage

Serves 6.

1   medium red cabbage, shredded
2   tablespoons finely minced onion
2   cups peeled and thinly sliced tart apple
3   tablespoons cider vinegar
2   tablespoons butter
1¼   teaspoons salt
¾   cup grape or red currant jelly
½   cup water, if necessary

Mix all ingredients except the water together, and cook in a heavy saucepan over low heat for 1 hour, stirring occasionally. Add water if it becomes too dry. This is good with game or pot roast.

> *Red flannel under-cloth, white orlon net covers. Pine cone Christmas trees. Silver candlesticks. Base of trees wreathed in holly, kumquat, etc., with miniature peppermint canes. Dining room table set with net cloth of cardinals over red flannel, a Christmas tree of boxwood, tied with tiny red satin bows. Silver foil butterflies and candlesticks. Food set out on table, then sat at small tables.*
>
> ~ JWS – 11/22/1965

Wild Rice and Mushroom Casserole

Serves 4 to 5.

1   cup wild rice
1   can beef consommé
2   tablespoons butter
½   pound mushrooms

Wash the rice, and remove any chaff. Place rice in a broad shallow casserole, cover with the consommé, and allow it to soak for 3 hours. Meanwhile, preheat the oven to 350°. Bake the rice covered for 45 minutes, adding a little water if it becomes too dry. Clean and slice the mushrooms, and sauté them in 1 tablespoon melted butter. Add the mushrooms and the extra tablespoon butter to the rice, and stir in gently with a fork. Uncover the rice and allow it to sit in the oven at 300°, until it has completely dried out and all the liquid is absorbed.

PLUM PUDDING WITH HARD SAUCE This makes 3-6 puddings, depending on the size of your molds.

PLUM PUDDING

1	pound raisins
½	pound currants
¼	pound candied citron
1	tablespoon candied orange peel
	(or substitute 1 tablespoon orange marmalade)
½	cup brandy or dark rum
1	pound best beef suet
4	eggs, lightly beaten
1	pint molasses
1	pint buttermilk
6	cups all-purpose flour
1	teaspoon baking soda
1	teaspoon salt
2	teaspoons cinnamon
½	teaspoon cloves
½	teaspoon allspice
1	teaspoon nutmeg

The day before making the pudding, mix the raisins, currants, citron, and orange peel or marmalade together, and cover it with the brandy or dark rum. Let it soak overnight. The next day, chop the beef suet fine. You may want to freeze it overnight and then chop it fine or grate it with a coarse grater. Stir in the eggs, molasses, and buttermilk. Sift the flour with the soda, salt and spices, and stir it gradually into the other ingredients to make a stiff batter. Add the fruits last. Grease your molds, and fill them ⅔ full with the mixture. Put the molds into a deep kettle with boiling water nearly as high as the top of the mold. Steam for 4 to 6 hours, adding water as necessary. When done, the pudding will spring back when pressed with a finger. Turn the puddings out to cool.

It is best to order the beef suet in advance from your butcher. Ask for the best suet with all the fiber removed. You can purchase a manufactured pudding mold. We use tall cylindrical cans that we've saved during the year. The bottom of the can is removed after the pudding is baked, and the pudding can be pushed out the other end. The puddings can then be cut into round slices for serving.

HARD SAUCE

½   cup butter, softened

1   cup confectioners' sugar

½   teaspoon vanilla extract or brandy

Cream the butter and sugar well together, and add the vanilla or brandy to flavor.

To serve the pudding, cut into serving slices. Warm them in a double boiler or microwave oven, and set each slice on a dessert plate. Pour brandy into a metal ladle. Hold the ladle over a burning candle, until the brandy is warm. Then ignite it, and pour the burning brandy onto the pudding. Pass the Hard Sauce at the table.

The author and her grandmother ~ December, 1954

CHAPTER VIII
JANUARY

A Game Dinner for Eight

CRAB SOUP

ROAST QUAIL WITH PORT SAUCE

BEST BAKED ORANGES

PERFECT SPOON BREAD

STEAMED GREEN BEANS

APPLE DUMPLINGS

Although my grandfather, Pop (as we called him), was a native of New York City, his fondest memories were of his three boyhood years and subsequent summers spent at Folly Farm, his family's country property in the Berkshire Mountains of western Massachusetts. Pop writes that his father, a city dweller all his life, wanted to try the "delightful" life of an agriculturalist, "one who by the plow would partly thrive, but he would neither hold nor drive." (This was Pop's play on Benjamin Franklin's famous quote in *Poor Richard's Almanac*.) In fact, throughout his life, Pop was happiest in the role of gentleman farmer. In later years (when their North Carolina mountain house was truly in the country), he could spend whole days cultivating the vegetable plot on his tractor, tending the berry garden, and fishing in the mountain lakes; at those carefree times, he probably felt he was back at Folly Farm.

The years on Folly Farm shaped Pop to a great extent, and inspired in him a lifelong love of the outdoors. In his memoirs of those days, which he titled "The Days of a Boy," he writes with obvious affection about the seasonal tasks of a farmer: planting and harvesting the crops; butchering and curing the meat. But the passages in which he expresses the greatest detail and delight are those related to nature. He savored the seasonal pleasures of the New England countryside: walking the woods, the "great pines and hemlocks, interspersed with enormous old chestnuts"; ice fishing in the winter for perch and pickerel; learning to stalk like an Indian after the deer in the woods; and identifying and observing the grouse, red-tailed hawk, and waterfowl that passed through Folly Farm.

A collection of ceramic mushrooms and Spode's Blackbird plates create a woodlands feel for the game dinner.

Family gatherings and food, especially that provided by the farm and its inhabitants, also figured prominently in Pop's memoirs. In describing the farm in November he writes:

> *On the table the gamey meats appeared, roasts of venison and grouse and wild ducks with all the trimmings of cranberries, and golden winter squash, and apple and pumpkin pies, with cider to drink, drawn fresh from the barrels in the cellar.*

Beginning in his childhood days in the Berkshires, and as long as his health permitted, Pop was an avid hunter and fisherman. No doubt, Charleston's proximity to the countryside, opportunities for shooting, and availability of plentiful game and birds attracted him to the area, as it had so many others during the various waves of northern migration.

Charlestonians and residents of the Lowcountry have always had an intense love of the land. In *A Carolina Rice Plantation of the Fifties*, Herbert Ravenel Sass writes:

> *The plantations and Charleston, in fact, constituted what was in practical effect a city-state unlike anything else that has existed in America—a compact and well-knit regional unit each part of which influenced the other so that the resultant society was neither purely rural nor purely urban but shared the characteristics of both town and country.*

Following the Civil War, planters could no longer count on their land as the economic resource it had been. As Virginia Christian Beach writes in *Medway*, "Having been stripped of their agricultural wealth by an invading army, plantation owners invested themselves, economically and emotionally, in one of their few remaining assets, the hunting grounds." Today, many plantations remain in the hands of Lowcountry families or have been bought and restored by northerners who as early as the late 1800s were attracted to the abundant game and the sporting lifestyle they found in South Carolina. Today's hunters are still passionate about the land, and, in the Lowcountry, are the group most dedicated to the protection of our rural areas.

In the 1960s my grandfather purchased acreage south of Charleston; he dubbed this hunting property "Juliette Plantation." There, and at the properties of friends, he hunted for deer, doves, and waterfowl. Gran's repertoire included a number of recipes for all the game that might find its way to a Charleston table.

My grandfather died at the relatively young age of 71. Crippled for many years by extreme osteoarthritis, he was unable to enjoy the outdoors during the last decade of his life. But his hunting friends never forgot him, or my grandmother, and continued to bring them birds, duck, and venison for many years. Well into the 1980s—during our Christmas morning ritual of opening gifts with the children in the drawing room—we often heard the doorbell ring around ten o'clock. Gran would answer the door, and there would be one of Pop's most loyal hunting buddies, with a gift of game or waterfowl.

In Charleston, the hunting seasons still rule the calendars of many Lowcountry families. Parties given on the first or last day of duck or dove season will be lacking many a huntsman, who would not miss that day in the field or duck blind.

CRAB SOUP

Makes 6 cream soups or 8 bouillon cups.

2	hard-boiled eggs
2	tablespoons flour
2	tablespoons butter, softened
	Grated rind of ½ lemon
3	pints milk, scalded
¾	pound crabmeat
½	cup cream
2	teaspoons Worcestershire sauce
1	cup Sherry or Madeira
	Salt and pepper to taste

Into a large heavy saucepan rub the yolks of the hard-boiled eggs to a paste with the flour and butter. Add the grated lemon peel and the whites of the eggs which have been put through a ricer, or grated. Add the hot milk to the mixture, stirring constantly. Cook about 5 minutes on low heat. Add the crab and bring to a boil. Stir in the cream, Worcestershire, Sherry or Madeira, salt, and pepper. Do not allow it to come back to the boil.

> *Cousin John is anxious for some shooting, so I have Kramer Nimitz* [a local hunting guide] *lined up. He says he will loan John one of Pop's guns for whatever kind of shooting he wants to do. I should imagine ducks, but that week every type of shooting will be open—doves, marsh hens, quail and wild turkey.*
>
> ~ JWS – 11/4/1972

Roast Quail

Serves 6. If using wild quail, you will often need two small birds per person.

Quail

6	quail
½	cup lemon juice or cognac
1	teaspoon salt
¼	teaspoon mace
6	tablespoons herb butter (see below)
12	seedless red grapes
6	tablespoons butter
½	pound mushrooms
1	bay leaf
6	sprigs parsley
½	teaspoon freshly ground pepper
1	ounce Madeira wine

Preheat oven to 400°. Rub quail all over with lemon juice or cognac, including inside the cavity. Season each quail with salt to taste and a pinch of mace. Fill the cavity of each quail with a tablespoon of herb butter and 2 grapes. In a shallow earthenware or enamel casserole, or a heavy roasting pan large enough to hold the quail close together, make a bed of the butter, mushrooms, bay leaf, and parsley, and season it with salt and pepper. Set the quail on the seasonings. Reduce the oven to 350°, and roast the quail for 25 minutes. Add the Madeira, and cook an additional 10 minutes. Serve the quail with Baked Fruit or Baked Oranges, and pass the Port Sauce.

Herb Butter

½	cup butter, softened
2	teaspoons dried mixed herbs (or 2 tablespoons fresh herbs, finely minced)

Cream the butter. Add fresh or dried herbs of your choosing, and mix well.

Port Sauce

About ¾ cup.

½	cup Port
	Pinch cinnamon
	Pinch nutmeg
	Salt and pepper to taste
10	ounces red currant jelly
1-2	teaspoons orange or lemon juice (optional)

In a heavy saucepan, combine the port and the seasonings, and cook over moderately high heat until it is slightly reduced. Stir in the jelly. Add the orange or lemon juice if desired. Serve warm to ladle over quail.

Best Baked Oranges

Serves 6 to 8.

3   quarts cold water
1   teaspoon salt
6   medium oranges
2   cups sugar
½   cup light corn syrup
1½   cups pineapple juice
3   sticks cinnamon

Salt the water and add oranges. Soak the oranges overnight. Next morning, drain and cover fruit with fresh cold water. Bring to a boil, then lower heat and simmer for about 1 hour, or until the skin of the fruit can be pierced easily. Drain and when cool enough to handle, cut oranges in half and remove core. Arrange the oranges as close as possible cut-side up in a shallow glass or ceramic baking dish. Preheat the oven to 350°. In a medium saucepan, make a syrup of the sugar, corn syrup, pineapple juice, and cinnamon sticks, and cook until it has slightly thickened. Pour over the oranges, and bake for about 3 hours, or until very tender. Baste frequently and turn the fruit from time to time.

Grapefruit may be fixed the same way—4 or 5 small grapefruit. This is equally good served hot or cold, and is delicious with ham, chicken, duck, or game birds.

Hunting on Kiawah Island, probably 1940s

PERFECT SPOON BREAD

Serves 4 to 6.

Spoon bread is a traditional southern side dish, and is essentially a souffléed cornbread. It's delicious served very hot, with a pat of butter.

2	cups whole milk
½	teaspoon salt
¾	cup cornmeal (preferably water-ground)
4	tablespoons butter
4	eggs, separated

Preheat oven to 350°. Butter a 1½ quart soufflé dish or casserole. Bring the milk to a boil in a medium saucepan, and add the salt. Pour the cornmeal slowly into the milk as it simmers, and stir constantly until smooth. Whisk it briefly if it gets lumpy. When the mixture thickens, add the butter, and stir until it melts and is incorporated. Remove from the stove, and beat in one at a time, 4 well beaten egg yolks. Beat the egg whites until they are stiff, but not dry, and fold into the cooled cornmeal mixture. Pour into the buttered soufflé dish, and bake 35 to 40 minutes at 350°. Time the spoon bread to serve immediately, and do not open the oven while it is cooking.

Can be doubled, in which case, bake it about 1½ hours.

> *My friend Richard Hutson brought me some doves this morning. Yesterday was the last of the dove season, and it is times like this I give thanks for Andrew who does not think it "off limits" to pluck and dress doves.*
>
> ~ JWS – 1/15/87

APPLE DUMPLINGS

Serves 4.

DUMPLINGS

6	medium-sized apples such as Rome, Cortland, Empire or Northern Spy
	Flakey Pie Crust (see page 176)
2	tablespoons butter
½	teaspoon cinnamon

Peel and core apples. Roll prepared pie crust very thin. Set apples onto the crust one at a time, and cut a square of pastry big enough to enclose the apple. Put a bit of butter and cinnamon inside the cored center of each apple. Wrap the pastry around the apple, bringing it together on top and leaving open vents where each edge comes together on the four sides. Apples may be frozen at this point. If unfrozen, bake at 350° for about 45 minutes until the crust is golden. If frozen, bake at 350° for 1 hour 15 minutes. Serve with sauce.

GRANDMOTHER WILES' SAUCE FOR DUMPLINGS

½	cup butter
1	cup sugar
¼	cup water
1	teaspoon vanilla

Mix the butter, sugar and water together in a small saucepan, and let come to a good boil. Add the vanilla and serve hot with apple or peach dumplings.

Sunday Afternoon Tea Party in the Drawing Room

SHRIMP PASTE SANDWICHES

HAM BISCUITS

CHEESE STRAWS

GUGELHUPF

WARM MARBLE CAKE

GREAT GRANDMOTHER'S SOUR CREAM SPICE CAKE

PECAN TEA CAKES

GRAN'S ALMOND COOKIES

There is something magical about the formal drawing room of Gran's house. Perhaps that is because it was used only for special occasions, such as Christmas morning, evening cocktails before a winter dinner party, or formal tea on a late, chilly afternoon. Always it has smelled delicious: of Christmas fir, of potpourri, or of the seductive aromas of a plethora of tea cakes. The elegant room, in its subtle tones of apricot and yellow, is as beguiling during the day when it is drenched in sunlight as it is at night, when its windows glow and draw eyes upward from the darkened street below. And, always, there is that "faint whiff" of potpourri as one passes the door.

For decades, one of Gran's unique ways of entertaining was to host a Sunday afternoon tea party in the drawing room. Tea parties, always planned for the cool months, were best in January or February. With a roaring fire in the fireplace, the room—with its delicate Adam mantel and beautiful Georgian woodwork—took on extraordinary warmth and cheer. I remember as a child dressing up for these elegant events and slipping—unnoticed by the grown-ups—from table to table to sample the special treats. My eyes were just at the level of the tabletops; the sight and smell of all those old-fashioned tea cakes was intoxicating.

The elegance of the afternoon tea party is reflected in the eighteenth century English silver tea urn and the Spode Maritime Rose china.

Out came the delicate silver tea urn and the antique porcelain cups. Gran, always seated in the wing chair in the corner of the room, served cup after cup of fragrant Chinese tea. For the men, there were fresh shrimp paste sandwiches, thin biscuits with salty slivers of Virginia ham, and crisp cheese straws to savor with their "brown liquor." Gran always maintained that Charleston men expected something more potent than tea on almost any social occasion, so Scotch and bourbon were served—even at a tea party.

Tea was the perfect accompaniment to the dazzling array of cakes. Among the treats were Gugelhupf (the lightly-sweetened German tea cake, studded with raisins and currants); Mother's Marble Cake (a fine-crumbed white cake with swirls of spice batter throughout); melt-in-your-mouth cookies like Pecan Tea Cakes; and Gran's own Almond Cookies. Guests often included three generations of family friends—from children to octogenarians—and all enjoyed this delightful alternative to a cocktail party.

> *I finally finished doing flowers yesterday. The various types of yellow and bronze chrysanthemums are always lovely in the room. The flower women had all kinds, and I have a few in my cutting area, so we are well fixed. The room looks well since it has been painted, and the mantel with the pink marble facing and the small plaques with the background of Wedgwood green are very unusual, and carry the color of the rug.*
>
> ~ JWS – 11/13/1969

SHRIMP PASTE SANDWICHES

This is a most delicious filling with a very delicate taste.

3	pounds fresh shrimp
½	pound butter, softened
1⅛	teaspoons celery salt
¾	teaspoon nutmeg
1⅛	teaspoons cayenne pepper
¾	teaspoon salt
	Homemade mayonnaise to thin it if desired
	Firm thin-sliced white bread (or you may serve as a spread on crackers)

Rinse the shrimp in a colander, then plunge them into boiling salted water and cook 5 minutes. Drain, remove shells and black vein in the back. Put the cooled shrimp through a meat grinder, or chop it very fine in small batches in a food processor. Cream the butter. Add the ground shrimp and beat until the mixture is smooth. Season with celery salt, nutmeg, cayenne pepper, and salt. Pack in a glass bread pan or dish and refrigerate mixture overnight. This can then be sliced thin and served with salad or can be softened and beaten again until it is of a consistency to spread on crackers or as a sandwich filling. If the paste is too stiff to spread easily, it can be thinned with 1 to 2 tablespoons of highly seasoned mayonnaise to soften it. After refrigerating, let it come to room temperature to spread easily.

To use shrimp paste in sandwiches, cut the crusts off slices of thin bread, and cut into triangles. Spread with the shrimp paste. This amount will make 50 thin sandwiches.

HAM BISCUITS

Make Ethel's Hot Biscuit, and let them cool to room temperature. Split the biscuits and if you wish, spread them with a little prepared mustard. Inside each biscuit, put a slice of salty, smoked Virginia ham, or if you prefer, baked ham.

Gugelhupf

1 cup whole milk
1 package dry yeast
3 cups flour, sifted
3 tablespoons sugar
1 teaspoon salt
3 eggs, slightly beaten
½ cup butter
⅔ cup raisins and currants mixed

Preheat oven to 325°. Scald the milk and cool it to lukewarm. Stir in the yeast until it dissolves. Mix sifted flour, sugar, and salt in a bowl. Make a well in the center and mix in the milk and eggs. Melt the butter and add it to the flour mixture, mixing well. Pour some boiling water over the raisins and currants to plump them up. Drain and shake dry, and mix them into the batter. Pour batter into a fluted tube mold or Bundt pan which has been well greased. Mold should be about ¾ full. Put in a warm place, cover, and let rise 1 to 1½ hours. Bake at 325° for 45 minutes to 1 hour. Turn out on a wire rack and sprinkle the top heavily with powdered sugar. Serve warm.

Great Grandmother's Sour Cream Spice Cake

3½ cups cake flour
½ teaspoon baking soda
3 teaspoons baking powder
2 teaspoons ground cinnamon
½ teaspoon ground cloves
1 teaspoon ground allspice
½ teaspoon ground nutmeg
½ cup butter
2 cups sugar
3 eggs, beaten slightly
1 cup sour cream
½ cup brandy
¼ cup powdered sugar for dusting

Preheat the oven to 375°, and grease and flour a 10-inch tube pan. Sift the cake flour with the soda, baking powder, and spices. Cream the butter with the sugar until light and fluffy. Add the eggs one at a time. Add the sour cream alternately with the flour mixture, and stir in the brandy. Pour the batter into the prepared tube pan, and bake for 50 to 60 minutes, or until a toothpick inserted into it comes out clean. Turn out onto a rack and sprinkle with powdered sugar, or cover with any good Seven Minute Frosting.

MOTHER'S MARBLE CAKE

1	cup butter, softened
2	cups granulated sugar
3	cups cake flour, sifted
3	teaspoons plus ½ teaspoon baking powder
1	cup whole milk
¼	teaspoon salt
6	egg whites
2	egg yolks, beaten
2	tablespoons molasses
1	tablespoon flour
1	teaspoon ground cinnamon
½	teaspoon ground cloves
¼	teaspoon ground allspice
¼	teaspoon ground nutmeg

Preheat oven to 300°. Grease and flour a 10-inch tube pan or 12-cup Bundt pan. Cream butter and sugar. Sift the cake flour with 3 teaspoons of the baking powder, and add to the butter/sugar mixture alternately with the milk. Add the salt to the egg whites, and beat until stiff but not dry. Fold the beaten egg whites into the batter. Remove one cup of the batter to a separate bowl, and add the 2 egg yolks which have been well beaten. Stir in the molasses, 1 tablespoon flour, ½ teaspoon baking powder, cinnamon, cloves, allspice, and nutmeg. Mix well. Pour some of the plain batter into the pan. Add a few spoons of the spice mixture, then more plain batter and the rest of the spice mixture. Don't spread the batter smooth; it should be dropped in irregular plops from a large kitchen spoon, in order to create the marbled effect. Bake for 10 to 15 minutes at 300°. Turn oven up to 350°, and bake for 45 to 50 minutes longer.

This cake is nice when made into two smaller cakes using two 6-cup Bundt pans. When making two smaller cakes, bake 15 minutes at 300°, then 20 to 25 minutes at 350°.

Pecan Tea Cakes

Makes about 50 cookies.

These little cookies have lots of different names such as Mexican Wedding Cakes and Sandies. This recipe is the best one I know—they melt in your mouth.

½   pound butter

4   tablespoons sugar

2   teaspoons vanilla

¼   teaspoon salt

2   cups pecans, chopped very fine

2   cups cake flour (measure before sifting)

½   pound powdered sugar, sifted

Preheat oven to 350°. Cream butter and sugar, and add vanilla, salt, nuts, and sifted cake flour. Mix well. Roll into small balls the size of large marbles. Bake on an ungreased cookie sheet for 20 minutes. Let cool for a minute or so before removing from the cookie sheet. Roll in powdered sugar while hot and again when they are cold. These are very fragile, especially when they are hot, so handle carefully.

You may chop the pecans in the food processor, but do so in small batches and be very careful not to over-process them or they will become oily. These cookies keep very well in a tin.

> *I put fresh potpourri in the drawing room containers and one bowl in the living room. It is faint and delicious, and the hostess was asked about it on the English tour. I love it—just a faint whiff as I go downstairs each morning.*
>
> ~ JWS – 11/2/76

GRAN'S ALMOND COOKIES

About 4 dozen cookies.

1   cup almond paste

1   cup butter

¼   teaspoon salt

1⅔   cups regular flour

1   cup powdered sugar, sifted

     Ground cinnamon as desired (ca. 2 teaspoons)

Preheat oven to 325°. Put almond paste in bowl of electric mixer, and beat until it is softened and smooth. Add butter and mix thoroughly. Work in salt and flour gradually. Chill dough thoroughly in the refrigerator, best overnight. Cut off thin slices of the dough and roll out on a floured board with hands to about a 3-inch length and the thickness of a pencil. You may leave them straight or shape into a half moon. Place on an ungreased cookie sheet and bake for 15 minutes. While cookies are baking, sift the powdered sugar, and add cinnamon to taste. Let the cookies cool slightly on the pan, then remove carefully while still warm and roll gently in the powdered sugar and cinnamon mixture

These cookies are so rich that they break easily if removed from the pan too soon. They are very crisp when cool, and are delicious with tea. They keep well in a tin.

CHAPTER X
JANUARY

A Small Luncheon Following Bookbinding Class

SHRIMP CONSOMMÉ

BEEF WITH WATERCRESS

RATATOUILLE À LA GRAND-MÈRE

DIVINE MUSHROOMS

CHOCOLATE POTS DE CRÈME

My grandmother was a voracious reader. In addition to poring over both Charleston's daily newspaper, *The Post and Courier*, and *The Wall Street Journal* each day, she was always engaged in several books at any given time. She was fascinated with history, current events, decorative arts, and literature. Classics, contemporary novels, and works of non-fiction on history, porcelain, and furniture were always stacked on the deep window seats in the living room and on the nightstand next to her bed.

Gran's fascination with books went even further, and included a decades-long involvement in bookbinding, papermaking, and paper marbleizing. She had studied binding in New York and Connecticut before moving to Charleston, and brought the craft with her when she moved, thus providing training for numerous young people in these ancient crafts.

My grandparents' love of the arts, architecture, and preservation led them to become involved with the Carolina Art Association, an organization which had been founded in 1857. In 1905, the Association opened the Gibbes Memorial Art Gallery (now known as the Gibbes Museum of Art). In 1932, the Association hired Robert N. S. Whitelaw as its first director. Mr. Whitelaw and his wife, Patti, had a profound influence on the arts and preservation over the following fifty years.

In his article on "The Carolina Art Association: Its First Hundred Years," published originally in *The South Carolina Historical Magazine*, Harold Mouzon writes, "Mr. Whitelaw was strongly of the opinion that the function of the Carolina Art Association was much broader than the development and operation of an art gallery. It should, he maintained, be a participant and a leader in every movement for the cultivation and preservation of beauty in the Charleston community."

The dessert buffet is set in the library, with contemporary Italian pots de crème on antique Crown Derby dessert plates.

Under Whitelaw's leadership, and at the request of the mayor, the Association managed the Dock Street Theatre—the small, exquisite reconstruction of an original eighteenth-century theater—and brought quality community theater to Charleston. Today that theater thrives with year-round local productions. It also serves as a venue in late spring for chamber music and theatrical productions of Spoleto Festival USA.

The Association created a Services Committee which undertook myriad civic projects. One of these projects was a proposal—which, in hindsight, seems remarkably prescient— for off-street parking adjacent to the retail areas of the city. Unfortunately, the City Council did not follow through on the suggestions, and Mouzon, even as early as 1958, noted that this was "a policy which many people now regret." The Committee also undertook a complete architectural survey of the city, and published the resulting book *This Is Charleston*. Not least of its accomplishments, this Committee founded the Historic Charleston Foundation—perhaps the single most important force in the preservation of Charleston's architecture and neighborhoods since 1947.

In 1962, my grandparents established the Dudley Vaill Memorial Bindery at the Gibbes Art Gallery. At the time, the bindery was one of the few hand binderies left in the United States, and the only one in the south. Named after Dudley L. Vaill, a noted bookbinder and author whom my grandparents had known in New England, the bindery provided training in bookbinding and book restoration for interested students from Charleston and across the country. For many years, classes were taught by Inez Pennybacker, who hailed first from Connecticut and later from Maryland. Miss Pennybacker did restoration of rare books for the Beinecke Library at Yale University; she came to Charleston for six weeks in the fall and ten weeks in the winter to teach at the Gibbes.

My grandmother's collection on book arts was donated to the College of Charleston over a ten-year period beginning in 1979. The bindery was operated at the Gibbes until the 1990s when it was closed; the remaining equipment and resources were given to the College.

Each morning when Miss Pennybacker was in Charleston, Gran walked to the bindery where she worked on personal projects. For each of her three grandchildren one Christmas, she bound—and lined with marbleized paper—a set of journals from my grandfather's safaris to Africa in the 1950s. These two volumes are among my most treasured possessions.

Often, after a morning at the bindery, Gran would return to host a small ladies' luncheon. This menu might have been served at such a small lunch in the winter months.

*S*HRIMP *C*ONSOMMÉ

Serves 6.

1	pound fresh shrimp in shell
2	cans consommé
1	large slice of onion
3	tablespoons prepared chili sauce
4	tablespoons dry red wine or sherry
½	teaspoon minced parsley
½	teaspoon salt
½	teaspoon chopped thyme
½	teaspoon mild curry powder
2	medium tomatoes
2	tablespoons cream

Peel, clean and de-vein the shrimp, and set aside. Heat the consommé with the onion slice, chili sauce, wine, parsley, salt, thyme, and curry powder. Peel and dice the tomatoes, and add them to the consommé. After the soup comes to a boil, add the shrimp and cook about 5 minutes until the shrimp are done. Before serving remove the onion slice and stir in the cream.

*B*EEF WITH *W*ATERCRESS

6	pound rib eye of beef
2	bunches watercress

Have beef at or close to room temperature. Preheat the oven to 300°. Roast 1 hour and 30 minutes. Then turn off oven and let stand 15 minutes longer. This gives a perfect medium rare meat. For a 7-pound roast, cook 1 hour and 45 minutes. Garnish the platter with bunches of fresh crisp watercress.

Gran very often served plain rare roast rib eye of beef, either hot or at room temperature. It was a great counterpoint to the rich creamed dishes such as Divine Mushrooms, Noodles Romanoff or Escalloped Oysters that often accompanied it. This is her recipe for perfectly roasted rare rib eye. These days I often substitute a tenderloin of beef, as I think guests prefer the leaner cut of meat.

RATATOUILLE À LA GRAND-MÈRE

½	cup plus 2 tablespoons olive oil
1¼	cups chopped red onion
1	bay leaf
2	cloves garlic, minced
1	teaspoon each of dried oregano, thyme, and basil
1	tablespoon chopped fresh parsley
1½	pounds eggplant
4	cups sliced zucchini
4	cups sliced yellow squash
¾	pound whole green beans
28	ounces canned Italian whole plum tomatoes
3	tablespoons catsup
2	tablespoons Worcestershire sauce
1	teaspoon salt
½	teaspoon coarsely ground black pepper

In a 10- to 12-inch sauté pan, cook the onions and herbs in 2 tablespoons of the olive oil until the onion is translucent. Remove the herbs and onion and set it aside. Peel eggplant and cut into ½-inch slices and then into chunks. Slice the zucchini and yellow squash into ¼-inch slices. Drain the tomatoes, reserving the juice. Add the remaining olive oil to the pan as needed, and sauté the eggplant, squashes, and green beans separately. Arrange each of the sautéed vegetables and the tomatoes in layers in a large earthenware or ceramic casserole, with the onion/herb mixture sprinkled between each vegetable layer. Deglaze the pan with the juice remaining from the canned tomatoes. Flavor it with the catsup, Worcestershire sauce, salt, and pepper. Cook this down until it thickens slightly, stirring constantly, and pour it over the dish. Bake at 350° for at least 1 hour.

Serves 8 to 10.

This is even better reheated. It can be served hot or at room temperature, and it freezes well.

*D*IVINE *M*USHROOMS

Serves 8 to 10.

2½ pounds fresh mushrooms
¼ pound butter
2 tablespoons herb butter
1½ pints sour cream
2 rounded teaspoons Dijon mustard
1 tablespoon finely grated onion
2½ tablespoons flour
    Salt to taste
    Dash of Tabasco sauce
2 tablespoons red wine
    Sprinkle of mace
    Chopped parsley

Clean mushrooms with a damp paper towel. Leave them whole or quarter according to their size. In a heavy pot, large enough to hold all the mushrooms, melt 2 tablespoons of the butter and 1 tablespoon of the herb butter. Add half the mushrooms. When the liquid starts to come out, add the rest of the butter, the herb butter and the other half of the mushrooms. Allow the mushrooms to cook for about 30 minutes, then remove them to a large shallow earthenware or ceramic casserole. Continue to cook down the mushroom liquid until it has reduced by half. Meanwhile, in a double boiler, mix the sour cream, mustard, grated onion, flour, salt, and Tabasco. Stir the mixture over hot water until it thickens. Add the remaining mushroom juice and the red wine. Pour the sour cream mixture over the mushrooms in the casserole. At this point you will need to keep the dish hot in a warm oven. But it requires no further cooking. Before serving, mix the sauce well through the mushrooms, and sprinkle with mace and a little chopped parsley.

This is good with any plain meat—super with game and beef. It is time-consuming to clean the mushrooms. You may clean them in advance and store the whole mushrooms in plastic bags in the freezer. When you are ready to prepare the dish, let the mushrooms partially thaw. Cut them in quarters if desired and proceed with directions. It will easily keep warm in the oven for 30 minutes.

HERB BUTTER

¼ pound butter, softened
1 tablespoon chopped fresh parsley
⅛ teaspoon dried tarragon
1 tablespoon chopped fresh chives

Cream the butter and add the herbs, gently crushing the dried tarragon before adding it. This can be frozen for future use.

CHOCOLATE POTS DE CRÈME

Makes 6 custard cups.

3   ounces unsweetened chocolate

1½   cups whole milk

½   teaspoon vanilla

3   egg yolks

¾   cup powdered sugar

½   teaspoon vanilla

Preheat the oven to 250°. Melt the chocolate in the top of a double boiler or in a heavy sauce pan. Add the milk and let mixture cook for a few minutes. Remove from heat and stir in the vanilla. Beat the egg yolks until thick and lemon colored, and add the sugar, mixing well. Slowly add the egg yolk mixture to the chocolate, stirring constantly. Fill small custard cups with the mixture. Set the cups into a shallow pan (such as a roasting pan), and fill with hot water about ¾ of the way up the custard cups. Bake for about 35 minutes. To test for doneness, tip one container slightly. Custard should be firm, but not hard. Chill for at least 2 hours before serving. Serve with whipped cream, slightly sweetened with sifted powdered sugar and a few drops of vanilla.

Tomorrow I am having a luncheon of fourteen. I don't think it is one of my star menus, as I got lost in the trees of various people's diets. But I am having a rib-eye of beef, cold, a big casserole of escalloped oysters, a green salad and an aspic salad, and three kinds of pots de crème—chocolate, vanilla and ginger.

~ JWS – 11/4/67

Stovetop Chocolate Pots de Crème

Serves 10.

1	pound sweetened dark chocolate
2	cups whole milk, scalded
6	egg yolks
1	tablespoon sugar

Melt chocolate in the top of a double boiler. Add the hot milk. Beat the egg yolks with the tablespoon of sugar until thick. Pour over the yolks the hot milk and chocolate mixture. Stir well and return to the double boiler. Continue to cook, stirring constantly, until the mixture is very thick. Pour into custard cups or pots de crème and chill several hours or overnight. Serve with Mocha Sauce (page 85).

An Elegant Winter Dinner

CREAM OF TOMATO SOUP

VEAL MARSALA

NOODLES ROMANOFF

STEAMED BROCCOLI

HOT CHOCOLATE SOUFFLÉ WITH MOCHA SAUCE

Charleston experiences just enough winter to allow its residents to enjoy a change in seasons. Snow falls rarely—perhaps once every few years. Clear, cool days are the winter norm, and encourage outdoor activities: brisk walks along the High Battery and around the city where the camellias are in bloom, their red, pink, and white blossoms visible behind gates and over garden walls; oyster roasts at country properties where city dwellers in tweeds come for the day to savor the salty bivalves; and bird or deer hunts, in evidence in the woods and along the rivers. Even January and February bring sunny, warm days when one can sail, ride horses, or play golf. And, most importantly, the social season is in full swing.

I've heard it said that the single greatest catalyst of change in the history of the south was the invention of air conditioning. While many Charlestonians still leave the city in the hot summer months—heading to New England, the North Carolina mountains, or the nearby beaches such as Folly, Sullivan's Island, or the Isle of Palms—far more today are able to remain in Charleston year-round in some level of comfort, thanks to the ubiquity of air conditioning. In spite

All went well and much conversation & laughter. Ben full of conversation as always—wild turkeys & S.C. politics.

~ JWS – 3/29/1974

Wedgwood plates and amethyst cased glass enhance the setting for an elegant winter dinner.

of this innovation, however, the height of the social season in Charleston is still from October through May. Full-time and part-time residents, guests, and tourists seem to agree that these relatively mild months are the Lowcountry's best. And some say the winter's days and rituals—the delicious food, crackling fires, and bonhomie—are best of all.

Gran was most noted for her large parties—luncheons and supper parties in the house or garden for twenty or thirty guests. But her party books record a constant stream of smaller parties for six or eight. These were given often to entertain close friends, other times to honor a special guest or a newcomer to the city. To Gran, it was just as important to have a congenial and interesting group as to have delicious food and an attractive table. Her notes cite both successes and failures in the art of conversation at the various events.

In the rush of life today, most of us don't make time to invite close friends or small groups to gather for dinner. But so often as I sit down to a good meal with my family, I am reminded how relatively easy it was to put together. I realize that with just a bit more attention to details and appearances, I could be sharing it with friends.

It's easy to make excuses—lack of help in the kitchen; a demanding job outside the home—but with some planning and organization, any of us can put together a tasty meal, a comfortable table, and a congenial group to enjoy it.

This is one of my favorite menus for a winter supper party. While the Veal Marsala may seem prohibitively expensive for a large group, it is reasonable (and simple) to prepare for a small party. The Noodles Romanoff is always a hit, and the hot chocolate soufflé is sure to elicit *oohs* and *aahs* from your guests.

Saturday was beautiful. Andrew had set up all of the tables in the living room on Friday, and most of the food had been done ahead and only had to be put together at the last. I had that in the dining room and everyone helped themselves. My friend Ralph had done the placecards. I just put camellias at the base of the candlesticks on each table, and a large red camellia with pin at each lady's place. All the food was eaten, several going back for seconds.

~ JWS – 2/17/1987

CREAM OF TOMATO SOUP

Serves 4 cream soups or 8 bouillon cups.

3	tablespoons butter
3	tablespoons minced onion
½	clove garlic, minced
4-5	good sized tomatoes
2	tablespoons tomato paste
3	whole cloves
2	cups good chicken stock
	Salt and pepper to taste
	Dash of cayenne pepper
½	cup plus 1 tablespoon heavy cream
	Minced chives

Melt the butter in a large saucepan. Add the onion and garlic and cook for 1 minute. Add the tomatoes which have been sliced or quartered with the skin on. Cook briskly for 5 minutes, then add the tomato paste, cloves, chicken stock, and seasonings. Stir over the heat until smooth and bring to a boil. After it has come to a boil, remove from the heat and strain the mixture. Return to the pan and simmer for 15 minutes more. Add ½ cup cream. Let soup heat, but do not boil. Stir in the additional tablespoon of cream just before serving, and sprinkle with the minced chives.

VEAL MARSALA

Serves 4 to 6.

2	pounds veal cutlet, cut thin
¼	cup flour
4	tablespoons butter (½ stick)
1	cup sweet Marsala wine
2	tablespoons sweet vermouth
2	tablespoons lemon juice
2	cups sliced mushrooms
1	clove garlic, mashed
2	tablespoons tomato paste
6-8	peppercorns
½	teaspoon salt

Preheat oven to 325°. Flour the veal cutlets. In a large skillet, melt the butter and brown the veal in it. Remove the veal to a shallow casserole. With the butter remaining in the skillet, deglaze the pan with the Marsala and vermouth. Add the lemon juice, sliced mushrooms, mashed garlic, tomato paste, peppercorns, and salt. Pour over the veal in the casserole. Bake covered for 1½ hours.

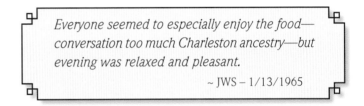

Everyone seemed to especially enjoy the food—conversation too much Charleston ancestry—but evening was relaxed and pleasant.

~ JWS – 1/13/1965

NOODLES ROMANOFF

½	pound wide noodles
1½	cups cottage cheese
1	clove garlic, minced
1½	tablespoons Worcestershire sauce
1½	cups sour cream
¼	cup minced onion
¾	teaspoon salt
	Dash Tabasco sauce
¼	pound grated Parmesan

Preheat oven to 350°. Boil the noodles in slighted salted water according to package directions until tender. Drain well. Combine all other ingredients except Parmesan, and mix well. Put in a shallow casserole and sprinkle with Parmesan. Bake 45 minutes.

HOT CHOCOLATE SOUFFLÉ

3   ounces sweetened dark chocolate
¼   cup cold water
⅛   cup butter
3   tablespoons flour
1   cup whole milk, scalded
⅓   cup granulated sugar
1   teaspoon vanilla
4   eggs, separated
    Butter and sugar for prepping soufflé dish
    Powdered sugar

Melt chocolate in the cold water in the top of a double boiler over hot, not boiling, water. Stir until chocolate is smooth. Remove from heat. In a separate heavy saucepan, melt the butter. Stir in the flour, and cook for two minutes, stirring constantly. Gradually add the hot milk, and stir until smooth and thick. Remove from heat and stir in granulated sugar, vanilla, and melted chocolate. Beat the egg yolks slightly and stir into the mixture. Beat the egg whites until they are stiff, but not dry. Fold whites into the chocolate mixture. Pour into a buttered and sugared 2-quart soufflé dish. Set it into a pan and add hot water to the pan about half way up the soufflé dish. Bake at 350° for 35-40 minutes, or until a knife inserted in the center comes out clean. Sprinkle with powdered sugar and serve with Mocha Sauce.

MOCHA SAUCE

½   cup very strong black coffee
    (you may use 2 tablespoons instant coffee
    dissolved in ½ cup water)
¼   cup granulated sugar
    Pinch of salt
2   egg yolks
½   cup whipping cream

Brew coffee, or make strong instant coffee mixture. Stir in the sugar and the salt until it is dissolved. Beat the egg yolks and add to the coffee mixture. Pour all into the top of a double boiler, and cook over hot water, stirring constantly, until it is thickened like custard. Remove from the heat, cool and place in refrigerator until ready to serve. Whip cream and fold it into the coffee mixture.

CHAPTER XII
MARCH

Breakfast on the Piazza

FRESH-SQUEEZED ORANGE JUICE

WADMALAW STRAWBERRIES WITH CREAM AND BROWN SUGAR

ETHEL'S HOT BISCUIT

PERFECT POPOVERS

ENGLISH MUFFIN BREAD

ASSORTMENT OF HOMEMADE PRESERVES

HOT COFFEE

I often wish I could time-travel and see Charleston through the eyes of a first-time visitor. For those of us who have lived here for a long time, perhaps the closest we can get to this is having houseguests, whose enthusiasm upon seeing Charleston for the first time is contagious. Gran had a constant stream of house guests throughout the year with the glorious spring being, of course, the most popular time for a visit. My father used to remark that my grandparents' house was like a "flyway," with northern guests touching down like migratory birds in the fall and spring.

Since the days when my grandparents first visited and stayed at the Villa Margherita at the edge of White Point Gardens, a plethora of hotels and bed and breakfasts has sprung up around the city. And since visitors have to eat, Charleston has experienced a proliferation of superb restaurants in the last two decades. But prior to that, houseguests and visitors dined to a great extent in private homes. That was certainly the case *chez Gran*. It is widely noted that in those days there were only two restaurants in town: Henry's, in the old market area, where one could get good, simple local seafood in a casual atmosphere; and Perdita's, near the waterfront, where one could dine more formally.

For centuries in Charleston, economics have had much to do with where and how people shopped for food and enjoyed their meals. When my grandparents moved to Charleston in the 1940s and for many decades after, Charlestonians had help in the kitchen; most had a cook for the big midday meal, and some had a cook in the evenings as well. Wages were modest; food was abundant. The

Aynsley and Spode china is mixed with nineteenth-century silver on the breakfast table. Morning sunlight on the new spring oak leaves provides an enchanting backdrop for this very Charleston setting.

market teemed with glorious local produce. The creeks, ocean, and forests were bounteous. People of that era had the habit of supplementing one another's pantries and freezers with the overflow of their crops or catch. My mother recalls that friends often brought shrimp, crab, tomatoes, venison, doves, and wild duck to the house. My grandfather frequently returned from an excursion in his small boat with fresh fish for our table.

As Charleston has become more popular and prosperous, real estate prices and the demand for residential or high-end commercial property have largely driven out the once-plentiful corner grocery stores and small eateries. I can remember from my childhood two corner stores located within two blocks of our house. One was Mr. Rhodes' store on Church Street; the other was Pete's on the corner of Meeting and Tradd Streets. (Both these buildings have long since been converted to private residences; the one which once housed Mr. Rhodes' store today has a shop on the first floor.) A charming high school essay—written in the 1940s by my mother—describes Pete's store:

> *Bananas hung on the awning frame of Pete's grocery store, ripening in the hot southern sun. The store itself was small and dingy, with cans and jars of almost everything imaginable piled from ceiling to floor. Penny candy stood for sale in large jars on the counter, and pop was always kept on ice for Pete's customers who came in to get cool after the heat of the street.*
>
> *Pete's was more than just a dingy grocery store; it was the neighborhood country club and meeting place. We girls...realized it was a man's domain. Eight or ten boys (our brothers and their friends) always sat outside the store on the broad window ledge and assumed an air of proprietorship, for this was really their club. ....It was Pete who kept the boys out of mischief, and Pete to whom they would go when they needed advice.*

In addition to these neighborhood shops were a number of small eateries which were very much in keeping with the flavor of the times. My mother remembers one at the corner of St. Michael's Alley and Church Street—in a building that now houses an art gallery—which served delectable she-crab soup, okra gumbo, and shrimp paste sandwiches. Also on Church Street, at the corner of tiny Longitude Lane, was another eatery. Called "Old Ironsides," the eatery operated out of a privately-owned clapboard house; it sported a rusted sign—which often swung in the breeze—of a clipper ship under full sail. The owner made what my mother and grandmother remember as the most delicious, crisp, light waffles and served them to guests in the living room. Even the venerable Brewton Inn, an early bed and breakfast establishment at the corner of Church and Tradd Streets, is now a private residence.

While Charleston today is resplendent—its houses and gardens in immaculate condition—many would argue that it has lost much of the charm of earlier days. Numerous houses—sometimes called "portfolio" or "trophy" homes because they are their owner's third, fourth, fifth, or even sixth residence—are empty most of the year. With so many owners absent, the vitality of the neighborhoods has waned. At times, the old city feels like a ghost town. And it's not just the little stores and eateries that have been displaced: young families with children have also been driven out by the skyrocketing real estate prices. The days of neighborhood children congregating at the corner store are a thing of the past.

One of the neighborhood dining traditions to disappear more recently was the "tearoom" that was held for a few weeks each spring—at the height of the tourist season—in the courtyard of the Confederate Home on Broad Street. (In Charleston, the term "tearoom" has come to mean a temporary dining venue where lunch is served to tourists and residents alike as a fundraiser for various service organizations.) While several churches and service organizations still host springtime tearooms around town—and serve fare that is quintessentially *Charleston* (shrimp paste

sandwiches, okra gumbo, and Huguenot Torte)—none is held in so gracious a setting as the old Confederate Home. Built in 1867 to house the mothers, widows, and daughters of Confederate soldiers, the rambling old building is one of Charleston's most atmospheric, with its rose-colored brick walls, shady courtyard, and three tiers of old wooden piazzas. The tearoom that was once hosted there is greatly missed.

Before Gran's houseguests struck out in the morning and worked up the appetite that eventually led them to the Confederate Home, they began the day with breakfast on the upstairs piazza. How magical it must have been for those from northern climes to step out of their bedrooms onto the piazza and into the full, fragrant glory of a spring day!

In the spring I can't get enough of the deep, red, luscious strawberries from nearby Wadmalaw Island, served with a splash of heavy cream and a sprinkle of brown sugar. Ethel's biscuits are wonderful in the morning; if they are left over from the night before, they can be reheated in the oven (a toaster oven is fine, but no microwave please). Pop's Popovers are easy and quick, and the English Muffin Bread makes delicious toast. Any of the above, of course, requires a selection of homemade jams, put away the previous summer. My standbys are strawberry, raspberry, and peach, but I often make plum, apricot, or blackberry as well. Add a couple of cups of strong, fragrant coffee, and your houseguests are ready to strike out on their sightseeing.

> *Today I am trying to do some "fiddling jobs," but the upstairs porch is so inviting, that I shall be hard put not to just give up and sit there and read.*
>
> ~ JWS – 5/17/87

PERFECT POPOVERS

⅓ cup all-purpose flour

⅛ teaspoon salt

2 eggs

⅓ cup milk

1 tablespoon butter, melted

Stir together the flour and salt. Beat the eggs until frothy and stir into the flour mixture. Add melted butter, and mix all ingredients well. Pour into 4 individual popover pans which have been thoroughly greased. Place pans on a cookie sheet and set in a cold oven. Set oven at 375°, and bake for 35 to 40 minutes. Do not open oven while baking.

To reheat, place popovers in a paper bag and place in 425° oven for 5 minutes.

*E*NGLISH *M*UFFIN *B*READ

2 loaves.

2	tablespoons dry yeast
6	cups all-purpose flour
1	tablespoon sugar
2	teaspoons salt
¼	teaspoon baking soda
2	cups whole milk
½	cup water
	Cornmeal as desired

Combine the yeast, 4 cups of flour, sugar, salt, and baking soda in a bowl. Heat the milk and water together to 115°. Add the liquids to the dry ingredients, and mix well. Stir in the remaining 2 cups of flour, and stir to form a stiff, but sticky batter. Spoon the batter into 2 loaf pans that have been greased and sprinkled with cornmeal. Sprinkle more cornmeal on top as desired. Cover the loaves with a damp tea towel and allow them to rise in a warm place for 45 minutes. Meanwhile, preheat the oven to 400°. Bake the loaves for 25 minutes. Remove from the pans immediately and cool on a rack.

This is an easy batter bread that requires only one rising, done in the pans. It makes delicious toast.

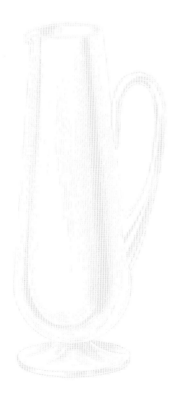

CHAPTER XIII
MARCH

Supper Before the Tours

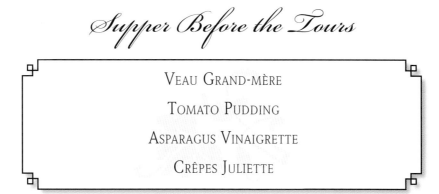

VEAU GRAND-MÈRE

TOMATO PUDDING

ASPARAGUS VINAIGRETTE

CRÊPES JULIETTE

efore they bought the house in Charleston, my grandparents lived full-time in Connecticut. Around 1940 they decided to look for a home in a milder climate, which they thought would be better for the sometimes fragile health of my mother and grandmother. According to my grandmother's story, they decided to look at Charleston, Savannah, and Mobile. My grandfather, being an architect, had a great interest in colonial architecture and preservation. The story goes that they arrived first in Charleston and stayed at the Villa Margherita, now a private home at the edge of White Point Gardens.

The villa and its setting—wonderfully described in *200 Years of Charleston Cooking* (edited by Lettie Gay and published in 1930)—are hauntingly evocative of that Charleston of an earlier time. Small wonder my grandparents fell in love with Charleston.

> *The Villa deserves to have an entire book written about its cookery, which has won for it an international reputation. It is, for some strange reason, better known in Europe than it is in this country. It is a quiet, restricted little hotel looking out over a park of live oaks and palmettos which curves along the edge of a blue bay. An occasional white-winged ship comes down this quiet bay, an occasional steamer crosses at a distance. But wild birds, ducks and gulls, and little sandpipers, are busy over it all day long.*

With an introduction from a mutual friend, they struck out with a Charlestonian for a tour of the city. Their guide told my grandfather that he had been able to arrange a visit to an early Georgian home, built in 1735, which he thought my architect-grandfather would find particularly interesting. As my grandparents were leaving—after touring the house and admiring its proportions

The spring supper table is set next to the herb garden with its brilliantly blooming azaleas.

and beautiful woodwork—the owner's wife happened to mention that her husband had decided to move back home, and they would be selling the house. No sooner had the front door closed than my grandfather put plans into motion to buy it. And, my grandmother would laughingly add, it was many years before they visited Savannah or Mobile.

It was the architecture that had originally attracted them to Charleston which, at that time, was a sleepy southern town where the homeowners were said to be "too poor to paint and too proud to whitewash." At the time of the American Revolution, Charleston had been the fourth-largest city in the new nation, behind New York, Philadelphia, and Boston. The surrounding plantations shipped crops of rice and indigo throughout the world, thereby generating tremendous wealth in the port city. Grand houses and public buildings were erected from the mid-eighteenth to the mid-nineteenth century. But after the War Between the States and continuing well into the second half of the twentieth century, the economy of Charleston declined; in fact, the city was preserved largely—and ironically—because of this very poverty. Whereas Americans elsewhere were building new cities, Charlestonians lacked the money to tear down the old buildings and erect more modern ones.

When my grandparents arrived, that tremendous trove of eighteenth- and nineteenth-century buildings was still largely intact. In 1920, a group of Charlestonians, led by Susan Pringle Frost, had begun to recognize the threat of losing valuable older buildings to the wrecking ball. They banded together to form a citizens group they named the Society for the Preservation of Old Buildings, now called simply the Preservation Society of Charleston. Arriving in the 1940s, my grandfather, a Yale-educated architect, was one of those who recognized the need for a preservation organization with a full-time professional staff. Toward that end, he became a key member of the group which founded the Historic Charleston Foundation in 1947. Along with many others, he went door-to-door to raise money for the purchase

in 1955 of the Nathaniel Russell House, which was to become the headquarters of the new Foundation.

The Russell House was purchased and opened to the public for tours. Early revenues went toward the Foundation's efforts to save individual historic structures. Eventually, the organization was able to establish a revolving fund, which culminated in the preservation of entire neighborhoods (beginning with Ansonborough, north of Market Street). To raise additional funds, the fledgling organization in 1948 started a series of tours of historic houses and gardens in the spring when the azaleas and wisteria were at their peak.

There was a time, including the period when my grandparents moved to Charleston, when the city had the reputation of being cold toward newcomers, when Charleston was said to be a city where it was "hard to be accepted." Today there are so many people moving here "from Off" that this reputation has largely disappeared. In any case, my grandparents never found that so. Perhaps because they devoted themselves to so many organizations in the community, because they were so determined to see not only the architecture of the city preserved but also its culture, arts, and way of life, they were welcomed by Charlestonians, and came to feel very much a part of the community.

In his book *Charleston: Azaleas and Old Bricks*, published in 1939, Samuel Gaillard Stoney describes the early tourist years between World War I and the Depression. "When Americans," he writes, "set out to discover their country, Charleston was to discover that she was an historical and artistic El Dorado…She had long been used to a certain decorous appreciation from a few discerning visitors, but here of a sudden was ecstatic admiration from crowds and crowds of tourists whose numbers jumped every year, and who for the most part knew nothing about the etiquette of touring." One can only imagine what Stoney would have thought of the tourist industry in Charleston today.

Stoney further describes those early waves of northerners and other newcomers who discovered Charleston—and the gracious plantations outside it—and made it their home:

> *About the same time that Charleston was suffering from one sort of visitor, another sort was benefiting her greatly. When the tourists of the boom were at their thickest, a number of people from other parts of the country saw in the town and in the splendid wreckage of the plantations the background for gracious and comfortable winter homes…Ever since that time this movement has gone steadily on throughout the Low Country, and Charleston has gained with it people who, in taking over the places of her lost planters, have at the same time acquired their loyalties to her.*

I like to think that Mr. Stoney would have included my grandparents in those who acquired loyalties to the city. I believe that they shared his sentiment when he counsels, "So if you would really care to know anything about her, come to Charleston…[and] wherever you wander and whatever else you do, try to feel as well as to see the town, because, like all other considerable human entities, Charleston is largely a matter of feeling."

Perhaps artist Elizabeth O'Neill Verner says it best in her book *Mellowed By Time*, published in 1941, when she states, "…we take them in when they love Charleston. That seems to be the standard we have set for taking strangers in and making them at home. It is the only requisite. They must love the city as we love it to become one of us."

Like everything in this city over the ensuing decades, Historic Charleston Foundation's efforts have grown and expanded. The Festival of Houses and Gardens continues to take place every March and April. Now spanning nearly five weeks, it includes lectures, oyster roasts, and educational luncheon lectures in addition to the house and garden tours. I am sure it has evolved far beyond what its founders imagined. Our house has been shown every year but one in the fifty-eight year history of the tours. As Gran approached her eighties, preparing for the tours became more and more difficult for her, even with my help; one year, I managed to convince her that she needn't show the house every single year. It was, however, more than she could stand not to be part of the tours, and every year after that the house was open. We continue that tradition today.

For years, my mother came every spring with different groups of ladies from southern California, where she lives. They filled the bedrooms and guest house and trooped off to every tour on the schedule. Supper was served early since the tours began at seven o'clock and ran until ten. I still tell people who come for the tours to go promptly, since it truly does take most of the three hours to visit the eight to twelve sites on each tour.

Veau Grand-Mère

Serves 4.

2	tablespoons butter
4	veal chops, cut 1-inch thick
	Salt and pepper to taste
8	small new potatoes
8	pearl onions
8	mushrooms
8	small strips salt pork
½	cup white wine
1	teaspoon glace de viande

In a heavy sauté pan, large enough to hold all the veal chops, melt the butter. Salt and pepper the veal and brown it in the pan over medium high heat. Cover, reduce the heat, and simmer the chops for 45 minutes. About 20 minutes before the chops are done, add the new potatoes and onions. In a separate pan, fry the strips of salt pork until crisp. About 10 minutes before the dish is finished, add the mushrooms and fried salt pork. When the meat and vegetables are tender, deglaze the pan with the wine and the glace de viande. Stir well to pick up the bits in the pan and use this as a sauce for the veal.

This is a nice dish as it includes its own vegetables.

The reception at the Russell House for the homeowners who were on the fortieth tour was most pleasant, although I did not stay long. It was inside and out, music in the garden. Patti had done the most beautiful flowers all through the house. I guess now the tours will go on, as the old houses are now in the hands of a younger generation, so they can make a fresh beginning.

~ JWS – 5/17/87

 Tomato Pudding

Serves 4, and can easily be doubled.

2   (10-ounce) cans tomato purée
½   cup light brown sugar
½   teaspoon salt
1   cup pieces of fresh white bread, crusts removed
½   cup melted butter

Mix the tomato purée, brown sugar and salt in a medium saucepan, and boil for 5 minutes. Put the bread pieces into a large bowl and pour the melted butter over it, mixing thoroughly. Add the tomato mixture. Mix well and pour into a 2-quart soufflé dish. Make the dish to this point 1 to 2 days before you need it. Cover and refrigerate. You must make this dish ahead as the point is for the bread to completely dissolve into the tomatoes and thicken the dish. No whole pieces of bread should remain. Preheat the oven to 375°. Bake the dish uncovered for 30 minutes, or longer if it goes in cold.

This is a fabulous side dish especially with plain grilled or roasted meats. It is unusual and adds beautiful color to the plate. Don't buy the super-soft white bread, but avoid very dense bread as well as it will not dissolve properly in the tomato sauce.

Vinaigrette Dressing

1   teaspoon salt
½   teaspoon freshly ground black pepper
⅔   cup olive oil
1   tablespoon white wine vinegar
½   cup red wine vinegar
1   tablespoon finely grated onion
2   tablespoons chopped fresh parsley

Stir the dry ingredients with a fork and add half the olive oil. Mix well and add the remaining ingredients, blending thoroughly.

This is delicious served over cooked celery, asparagus or Jerusalem artichokes. Steam the asparagus for about 3 minutes, chill and serve room temperature with the Vinaigrette Dressing.

CRÊPES JULIETTE

Makes about 30 crêpes.

PERFECT CRÊPES

1	cup sifted flour
2	tablespoons sugar
4	eggs
1	cup whole milk
1	cup water

Sift the flour with the sugar in a small bowl. In a larger bowl, beat the eggs with a whisk. Add the dry ingredients and beat the mixture until smooth. Add the milk and water gradually, and stir the batter until smooth. It will have the consistency of cream. Let the batter stand for at least 2 hours, or refrigerate overnight. If it becomes too thick on standing, thin with a spoon of milk or water. Heat a 5-inch well seasoned crêpe pan until hot. Coat it with a small amount of butter. Each crêpe takes about 1 ½ tablespoons batter. Measure that amount into a large kitchen spoon so you know how much to add for each crêpe. In this way you can avoid making two dips of the batter. Pour batter into the pan and quickly tilt and rotate the pan so that the batter runs to the edges and coats the bottom thinly and evenly. Return the pan to the heat for a minute or two. When the top of the crêpe is just set, lift the edge with a spatula to see if the bottom is a deep golden brown. Using your fingers, carefully turn the crêpe over. Brown the other side for about 30 seconds or until the crêpe is cooked. Do not overcook the crêpe, and turn it only once. Slide the crêpes onto a wire rack. Cool the remaining crêpes and as they cool, pile on top of each other.

The pan can be wiped out with a paper towel after the butter or oil melts and before baking the first crêpe. Alternatively, the first crêpe can be discarded. Do not grease the pan again during the baking of the crêpes. These freeze perfectly. Put a foil square between each crêpe, and freeze in stacks, wrapped carefully in heavy foil.

CRÊPES JULIETTE

Enough sauce for 4 to 8 crêpes.

8 lumps of sugar

1 orange

1 lemon

3 tablespoons unsalted butter, softened

1 ounce (2 tablespoons) of each of the following:

    Cointreau

    Benedictine

    Dark Rum

2 ounces (4 tablespoons) Grand Marnier

½ ounce (1 tablespoon) Kirsch Wasser

¼ cup granulated sugar

    Cognac for igniting

Rub 6 sugar cubes over the orange rind so as to saturate the sugar with the oil of the peel. Rub 2 sugar cubes over the lemon rind. Squeeze the juice of half of the orange, and strain it onto the sugar cubes. Crush until the sugar is melted, and mix it with the butter. Measure the different liqueurs and mix together.

To prepare at the table if you have a tabletop Crêpes Suzette pan:

Arrange all of the above and the crêpes on a tray. Heat pan over flame and add the butter/sugar cube/orange mixture. Using a fork and spoon, lay each crêpe into the pan, and turn it so that the mixture coats each side. Fold the crêpe in half and then into quarters, and push to the side of the pan while you prepare the others. When all crêpes are done, sprinkle them with the granulated sugar, then pour the liqueur mixture over all. When the crêpes have simmered for a few seconds, tilt pan to ignite. After the liqueur stops burning, serve on warm plates with sauce.

The Crêpes Juliette take some practice before you will be comfortable cooking in front of your guests. The following alternatives can be prepared in your oven in the privacy of your kitchen:

BROWN SUGAR CRÊPES

Serves 6.

12 crêpes
4 tablespoons butter
½ cup light brown sugar
    Coffee ice cream

Put 1 teaspoon brown sugar and ½ teaspoon butter on each crêpe. Fold crêpe in half, and arrange in a slightly overlapping layer in a buttered ovenproof dish. When all the crêpes are in the baking dish, dot with 2 tablespoons butter and 6 tablespoons brown sugar, and broil about 8 inches from the heat until the sugar is melted. Serve the crêpes warm with firm, rich coffee ice cream.

LEMON CRÊPES

Serves 4.

8	crêpes
¾	cup granulated sugar
2	teaspoons grated lemon peel
2	tablespoons butter

Fold crêpes in half and arrange in slightly overlapping layer in a buttered shallow ovenproof dish. Sprinkle with sugar mixed with the lemon peel. Dot with the butter. Broil about 5 inches from heat until sugar is melted and bubbling.

SAUCE FOR LEMON CRÊPES

½	cup butter
½	cup brandy
¼	cup Cointreau or Grand Marnier
2	tablespoons lemon juice

In a saucepan, melt the butter. Add the brandy and Cointreau or Grand Marnier and the lemon juice. Heat the sauce, stirring until well blended, and serve warm with the crêpes.

CHOCOLATE ORANGE CRÊPES

Prepare fresh orange sections with all the white membrane removed. Roll the orange sections inside a prepared crêpe. Garnish with whipped cream flavored with Grand Marnier, and shaved bittersweet chocolate.

A Country Picnic at Rockville

Brie and Water Biscuit with Artichoke Relish

Crudités – Carrots, Celery, Radishes and Olives

Shrimp and Crabmeat Salad

Deviled Eggs

French Bread

Mrs. Gwinn's Almond Cake

Tante's Shortbread

Billie Cookies

Even before downtown Charleston became busy and crowded with tourists, Charlestonians loved to escape to their country homes. In some cases, the "country home" was a formal plantation where guests might be invited for a weekend of shooting. In other cases, it was a simple cottage on one of the sea islands or creeks, where friends could spend time fishing and shrimping. Due to pollution, many states today have suffered the loss of fishing, shellfish harvesting, or beach going. In the South Carolina Lowcountry, however, waterways are (with occasional exceptions) still clean enough for locals to harvest and enjoy blue crab, oysters, and shrimp.

Unlike other parts of the country, where a weekend home may be hours away, lowcountry retreats typically can be reached in thirty minutes to an hour—the length of an average daily commute in many places. Wadmalaw Island, Edisto Island, and the breathtaking ACE Basin (named for the three rivers—the Ashepoo, Combahee, and Edisto—that define it) lie to the south; the pristine Santee Delta, Winyah Bay, and their associated plantations make

An English picnic hamper sits under the oak trees at the edge of Wadmalaw Sound with a salad of shrimp and crab from local waters.

up the spectacular landscape to the north. South Carolinians have always had a special love for the land, and we are fortunate that private landowners and organizations such as the Lowcountry Open Land Trust, the Coastal Conservation League, and others are working together to ensure that this landscape will be preserved for the future.

Not only do conservationists and most residents want to safeguard the environment, preserve scenic vistas, and ensure good hunting and fishing, but they also want to protect the traditional agriculture of the area. In recent years, many Charleston restaurants have touted the local produce they serve, such as Wadmalaw field greens and "Wadmalaw Sweets" (the local variety of sweet onion similar to the Vidalia or Maui Sweets found elsewhere). The succulent tomatoes grown on Johns and Wadmalaw Islands are prized not only when they are ripe and juicy, but also when they are still green; these find their way into local restaurants as fried green tomatoes, or into homes as wonderfully crisp green tomato pickle. (Mrs. Sassard's Iced Tomato Pickle and her Jerusalem Artichoke Relish, made locally and used in these menus, are still the best, and are readily available in area groceries.) Recently, however, restaurateurs report that finding fresh local produce is becoming increasingly difficult—another unfortunate consequence of the explosive development in the area.

I can still remember hearing, on my visits to Charleston as a child, the shrimp and vegetable peddlers calling out as they made their way down Church Street with their wares. "Swimpy, swimpy" was their familiar musical cry. I'd look out the window high on the third floor to see the shrimp man as he came down the street, pushing his wooden wagon full of fresh local shrimp. One of my favorite errands was accompanying my grandmother to Mr. Carroll's fish market at the corner of East Bay and Market Streets. For a young child from Ohio, seeing the local flounder, grouper, shrimp, and crab laid out on ice for display in the store

was an eye-popping experience. One of the stories my father loves to tell is how I, at age three, was introduced to my first oyster. It was during my father and grandfather's favorite winter ritual, which involved sitting on the back porch—oyster gloves, knives, and cold beer at the ready—and sharing a burlap bag full of fresh local oysters. In the company of these two oyster enthusiasts, I tasted my first briny, raw, lowcountry bivalve. Clearly, it made a good impression, for I still love oysters in all their manifestations: raw, roasted (steamed), or cooked in my great-grandmother's recipe for Escalloped Oysters.

When I moved to Charleston as a young adult in 1976, the market sheds were filled with the local farmers who brought their produce into town to sell. I remember my grandmother telling me proudly that Charleston had been very foresighted in saving its market while Savannah had torn hers down. That was the time when shops and restaurants were just beginning to be opened in one end of the market. Now the market contains only shops, restaurants, and vendors who come during the day to set up their booths for the tourists. Sadly, the locally-grown produce and lowcountry crafts are, for the most part, no longer sold there; one hopes that trend can be turned around in the future.

The basket ladies—weavers of the Lowcountry's traditional sweetgrass baskets—can still be seen at the market as well as at the corner of Broad and Meeting Streets. Their craft, brought to these shores by their forebears—the West African slaves—has been passed down through the generations. The intricately-coiled baskets were used on the plantations to separate the rice from the chaff; they continue to be made today as beautiful decorative items and popular souvenirs.

Gullah is the term used for the people, the culture, and the exotic, rhythmic language of the descendents of the former slaves. Their labor was the basis for the tremendous wealth of Charleston and the plantations; their rich culture has contributed immeasurably to the city and its environs.

In _Charleston: Azaleas and Old Bricks,_ Samuel Gaillard Stoney writes of the Gullah language:

> _It is in the air of a city made musical by the cries of Negro vendors of fish, or flowers, and the speech of blacks and whites that is, as I have said, pervaded with the richness or at least the recollection of its rhythm. You will find it at its most intense moments there on market days, under the tier of long old sheds that stretch from the Bay to Meeting Street, when 'Jeems' Islanders and people from 'Hongry Neck' have fetched in the parcels of vegetables, the chickens, and the little fagots of lightwood that are their stocks in trade. And you may get it in a more subdued form among the women who congregate on the broad pavements about the Post Office to sell their baskets of flowers wild and tame, and happily distract your attention from one of the ugliest buildings in Charleston._

In recent years, the City of Charleston and some of the surrounding towns have, in renewed recognition of the value of our local farmers, started their own farmers markets. The fresh produce market in downtown Charleston is flourishing in its current home in Marion Square; the local farmers do brisk business there on Saturdays, selling strawberries, butter beans, corn, and tomatoes in season.

In the late 1940s and 1950s, my grandparents had a small house in Rockville on Wadmalaw Island, a remarkably unspoiled sea island where local farming can still be observed. Rockville itself is a dreamy, nineteenth-century village at the tip of the island, with simple white clapboard houses nestled among old oaks hung with Spanish moss. My mother remembers summers when they lived on what could be found in Rockville: shrimp from the creek, tomatoes from roadside stands.

When I visited Charleston as a teenager, Johns Island, and much of James Island, were still largely rural. The road traversing James Island to Folly Beach meandered past trees, open space, and the occasional vegetable or basket stand. Today, the same road winds past strip malls, neon signs, gigantic stores, and asphalt parking lots. As the area has grown over the last decades, development has changed the face of these nearby islands; the rural and agricultural lands have been pushed farther and farther out. One can only hope that the constant battle to preserve the rural areas and traditional agricultural practices will ultimately be successful.

But for now, Rockville and other country communities maintain a sense of what is truly the Lowcountry: grand oak trees with their Spanish moss, creeks where one can still catch local shrimp and oysters, and above all the peace to enjoy it!

> _The town is still overflowing with tourists; the traffic is wild. The newspapers full every day of the troubles on the bridges and the roads from Summerville and the islands, and building continues._
>
> ~ JWS – 5/17/86

SHRIMP AND CRAB SALAD

Serves 8.

4	pounds raw shrimp
2	hard-boiled eggs
½	bunch celery
½	cup Mother's Boiled Dressing
1	cup homemade mayonnaise
1	pound crabmeat

Boil shrimp and pick clean, removing the vein. Hard boil the eggs, and let them cool. Chop the celery, and the hard-boiled eggs, or grate the eggs with a coarse grater. Combine the boiled dressing and the mayonnaise and mix it with the shrimp and crabmeat. Stir in the celery and hard-boiled egg. Serve on lettuce leaves, and if desired, drizzle with Snappy Salad Dressing.

MOTHER'S BOILED DRESSING

1	teaspoon salt
1	tablespoon sugar
2	heaping tablespoons all-purpose flour
2	egg yolks
1	cup whole milk
1	cup cider vinegar
1	tablespoon butter
	Dry mustard and white pepper, to taste

Mix the salt, sugar and flour in the top of a double boiler. Add the egg yolks, beaten slightly, and mix well. Stir in the milk and vinegar, and add the butter. Cook in the double boiler until dressing is thick.

This keeps well in the refrigerator in a jar.

*M*RS. *G*WINN'S *A*LMOND *C*AKE

This is a delicious and fragrant almond pound cake. Mrs. Gwinn, was a neighbor of the Wiles family in Huntington, West Virginia. According to Gran, she was originally from Kentucky, and "had cream that rolled back like velvet."

1	pound almond paste
1	pound butter, softened
1	pound sugar, less ½ cup
10	large eggs
1	pound cake flour, sifted
½	pound citron, finely grated (optional)
¼	pint apple brandy (or up to ½ pint)

Preheat oven to 325°. In an electric mixer, beat the almond paste until somewhat smooth. Add the whites of two of the eggs one at a time, and continue beating until quite smooth. Add the softened butter and cream it with the almond paste, then add the sugar and cream thoroughly. One at a time, add the two egg yolks and the remaining whole eggs, beating well after each addition. Mix in the brandy. Gradually add the sifted flour and mix well. Pour into a 12-cup Bundt pan or 10-inch tube pan which has been greased and floured thoroughly. Bake for 1 hour or until the cake tests done. Cool in the pan for a few minutes, then turn onto a rack to finish cooling.

TANTE'S SHORTBREAD

Tante Gould was a cousin of my grandfather Staats, and a talented cook judging by all the recipes I find attributed to her. Gran described Tante's mother, Cousin Grace, as "lively as a cricket until the day she died." I remember visiting Tante late in her life in her New York apartment. These cookies have always been a favorite, especially at the Christmas season.

1	cup butter, softened
½	cup light brown sugar
1	teaspoon vanilla
2	cups flour
¼	teaspoon salt

In an electric mixer, cream the butter and the brown sugar thoroughly. Mix in the vanilla. Add the flour and salt gradually, mixing well. Roll the dough into a long roll, and chill several hours or overnight. Slice thin and bake on an ungreased cookie sheet 8 to 10 minutes at 400°.

*B*ILLIE *C*OOKIES

About 45.

This recipe came from my paternal grandmother's delightful cook Billie Hunter. It was a special treat whenever the grandchildren visited.

1   cup butter, softened
6   tablespoons dark brown sugar
6   tablespoons granulated sugar
1   egg
½   teaspoon vanilla
1   cup plus 2 tablespoons flour
½   teaspoon salt
½   teaspoon baking soda
1   cup finely chopped pecans

Preheat oven to 325°. Cream the butter. Gradually add the sugars and beat until creamy. Beat in the egg and vanilla, mixing well. Sift the flour with the salt and baking soda, and add it gradually to the butter mixture. Stir in the chopped pecans. Drop by teaspoons, well apart on a greased cookie sheet and flatten slightly. Bake about 10 minutes. Remove from the cookie sheet while still hot, and let them cool thoroughly on a rack.

Phil and Juliette Staats ~ Sea Island Picnic, 1965

Chapter XV
April

A Spring Luncheon on the Terrace

Blanquette of Veal

Salad of Bibb Lettuce, Avocado, and Parsley Dressing

Hot Sourdough Rolls

Lemon Curd Tartlets

---

*I*t is difficult to imagine any place lovelier than Charleston in April. The spring flowers are at their peak, the air is soft and balmy, and, if you time things just right, the "no-see-ums"—those pesky tiny gnats that swarm here in the warm weather—can be avoided. A luncheon on the terrace is the best time to enjoy the blooms and the fragrant, bug-free air.

We are fortunate to have a small terrace at one end of the rear garden, shielded from view by a lush latifolia holly. The two outdoor tables there can each be set for four or six. In this private setting, one can enjoy the surrounding azaleas, the fragrance of the dwarf gardenias, and the view of the urn—framed by a pair of eighteenth-century Italian wrought-iron gates—at the garden's rear.

For special luncheons, we dress up "the girls"—the sculptures of the Four Seasons which grace the garden adjacent to the terrace. The sculptures are the work of Henry Mitchell, an American sculptor from Philadelphia who was a close family friend. Each of the bronze statues holds a basket; for parties in the garden, these can be filled with flower arrangements which trail over the girls' arms and skirts.

Henry Mitchell and his lively wife, Marian, were stationed in Charleston while he was in the Coast Guard during World War II. They became lifelong friends of the family, and, for a time, surrogate parents to me. After finishing Stanford University, I lived for two years in Vienna, Austria; one of the joys of that period was visiting Henry and Marian. I would take the overnight train from Vienna to their home in Milan, Italy, where Henry had his foundry; on weekends, we would often make the drive to their charming villa in Orselina, Switzerland. I remember so well the sunny villa with its terraces—adorned with Henry's sculpture—looking down on the Lago Maggiore. Evenings were celebrated with their international friends of all ages; on our trips to restaurants we were always accompanied by their toy poodles, Risi and Bisi. What fun we had!

The refreshing lemon tarts are irresistible on Mintons and Dresden dessert plates. The landscaping surrounding the terrace ensures privacy.

Gran had commissioned Henry to do the sculpture of the Four Seasons for the garden; in 1980, he and Marian traveled to Charleston for the installation. They had flown with the statues from Milan to Philadelphia, and he was not feeling well as they began the drive to Charleston. Henry persevered through the installation of the sculpture, but immediately went into a local hospital where he passed away two weeks later of pneumonia. Two years after his death, Marian gave Gran a small pair of Henry's unicorn sculptures, which today stand on pedestals and greet guests on the walkway to the terrace.

A garden luncheon might include this Blanquette of Veal—along with a fresh green salad of Bibb lettuce, avocado, and parsley dressing. The rich, tangy lemon curd tart makes a perfect warm weather dessert. The curd can be made well in advance and stored in the refrigerator, then assembled in the tart shells shortly before the luncheon.

Had luncheon in the garden at two tables for four.
A perfect day, and everyone seemed to enjoy food.
Put some small round tables on terrace, and had
food there. Dessert was passed.

~ JWS – 11//25/1963

Catherine Staats Huffman ~ Spring tours, 1961

Blanquette of Veal

3	pounds veal cut into bite-sized pieces
12	small carrots
18	pearl onions, peeled
1	teaspoon salt
¼	teaspoon white pepper
4	cups chicken stock
3	tablespoons butter
3	tablespoons flour
¾	pound fresh mushrooms, cleaned and sliced
3	egg yolks, slightly beaten
	Juice of 1 large lemon
¾	cup light cream

Soak veal cubes in cold water for 20 minutes. Pour off the water and place veal, vegetables and salt and pepper in a large heavy saucepan. Add 4 cups chicken stock. Cover the pan and bring the contents slowly to a boil. From time to time skim the foam that forms on the top. Let the veal simmer for an hour or so until it is tender. Remove the meat from the heat and keep it warm. Remove and discard the vegetables. In a large heavy skillet, melt the butter. Add the flour, and cook for 3 minutes, stirring constantly. Add one cup of the broth in which the veal was cooked, and bring to a boil. Add the mushrooms and simmer 10 minutes. Remove the pan from the heat and add a little of the sauce to the slightly beaten egg yolks. Blend together and add the juice of one lemon and the reserved veal. Any remaining stock in which the veal was cooked may be discarded. Stir in the cream. Reheat, but do not boil. Correct the seasonings as needed and serve with rice.

The blanquette may be made the day before up to the point of adding the cream. It may also be frozen before adding the cream. In either case, the cream is added as the dish is reheated. This is wonderful served with plain or herbed rice.

PARSLEY DRESSING

1	teaspoon dry mustard
1½	teaspoons salt
¼	teaspoon coarsely ground black pepper
1	tablespoon chopped fresh chervil (if not available, used leaves of celery heart)
⅓	cup red wine vinegar
¾	cup pure olive oil
½	cup chopped fresh parsley
1	tablespoon minced fresh chives

Mix the mustard, salt and pepper in a medium-sized bowl. Add the chervil or leaves of celery heart. Add the vinegar and gradually whisk in the olive oil. Stir in the parsley and chives.

This is especially delicious on a salad of soft leaf lettuce and avocado or of mixed greens. Mix the dressing well and store in the refrigerator several hours or overnight.

*L*EMON *C*URD

¼	pound butter, melted
2	cups granulated sugar
⅔	cup strained lemon juice
¼	teaspoon salt
5	whole eggs
3	egg yolks

Mix the melted butter, sugar, lemon juice and salt in the top of a double boiler, until well blended. Beat the whole eggs and egg yolks together slightly. Add the egg mixture to the lemon juice mixture, and stir constantly over hot water in the top of the double boiler until thickened, about 10 minutes. (Remember, it will thicken further as it cools.) Do not overcook.

This filling may be put in tightly sealed glass jars in the refrigerator, and will keep well for 4 to 6 weeks.

*L*EMON *T*ARTS

Prepare Flakey Pie Crust (see page 176). Roll thin and form into individual tart shells. Blind-bake the shells for 10 to 12 minutes at 425°, and when cool, add the lemon filling. Serve with a dollop of whipped cream, and garnish with a ripe raspberry and a mint leaf, or if you prefer, you may top it with meringue. If you top it with a meringue, finish it in a 325° oven for about 15 minutes, or until the meringue is golden.

You may also make this as a 9-inch pie instead of individual tarts.

CHAPTER XVI
MAY

A Spoleto Luncheon in the Garden

BOWLE

SALTED PECANS

CHARLESTON SHRIMP

RICE RING

BUTTERED SPINACH

ORANGE LAYER CAKE

*I*n 1977, Gian Carlo Menotti chose Charleston as the site for the Spoleto Festival USA, the American counterpart of his long-running Festival dei Due Mondi in Spoleto, Italy. Just as the setting of the Italian hill town enhances the original Spoleto Festival, so does the magical backdrop of Charleston enhance the new world version. Performances, given during three weeks in late May and early June, are held in handsome, historic theatres, churches, courtyards, gardens, and public spaces. But Charleston provides much more than a passive stage set to the Festival. Volunteers work on its many aspects, especially hospitality: fabulous, nearly-nonstop parties are given in private homes and gardens to honor distinguished artists, celebrate opening nights, and, generally, enjoy *la dolce vita*.

Gran had a number of friends who would visit each year during the Festival, immersing themselves in the opera, ballets, plays, and chamber music from mid-morning until late at night. Some of her New York friends were skeptical about coming to Charleston for the Festival, feeling that they had the best of music and the arts right where they lived. But the Spoleto Festival's strength is that it has always focused on spotlighting new artists or providing the opportunity for an established artist to debut in a new discipline.

Certainly, much of the magic of Spoleto comes in having the opportunity to go from your hotel or inn to a performance—and on to lunch, dinner, or cocktails in a private home—without ever climbing into a car. The early summer air is balmy; often one catches the sound of a voice or instrument wafting down a lane from a theater or rehearsal studio.

The Piccolo Spoleto Festival—the simultaneous, parallel festival sponsored by the city—offers more than 700 performances, many of them free, all over town, as well as almost-continuous events geared toward children and families. And the Spoleto finale each year is a symphony concert held on the banks of the Ashley River. Concert-goers spread their blankets and picnic suppers

The enormous oaks provide welcoming shade for the luncheon tables.

on the slope behind the ruins of the house at Middleton Place plantation; below them, on a grassy space nestled between the fabled Butterfly Lakes, is the orchestra. The river, noble oak trees, and surrounding marshes provide an almost surreally beautiful background; fireworks illuminate the night sky at the end of the evening.

Following the inaugural festival in 1977, the *Los Angeles Times* opined, "Charleston—lovely, sleepy, reticent, proud, historic Charleston—may never be the same again." For better or worse, those words have proved prophetic. And while Charleston can no longer be considered sleepy, it remains lovely, proud, and historic—and an increasingly popular destination for visitors from around the world.

As important as the Festival itself is to Charleston, it has brought even more to the day-to-day cultural life of our community. Beyond its annual three-week tenure, Spoleto sparked a renaissance in the arts that just keeps growing stronger. Ballet companies, a world class symphony orchestra, and above all a thriving movement in the visual arts are Spoleto's enduring gifts to the city that hosts it each year. Throughout the old historic neighborhoods—especially on Broad, Church, Queen, and East Bay Streets—a broad mix of galleries has sprung up. The tradition of regularly-held (and very popular) Art Walks has been established and taken hold. On a typical Art Walk, throngs of gallery-goers wander among the ten to twenty galleries included on that evening's walk, enjoying hors d'oeuvres and wine. The crowds spill convivially onto the sidewalks and into the streets, making the Art Walk a kind of moveable feast. This lively arts scene is doubtlessly indebted to the Spoleto Festival, whose presence over the decades has truly had a classic domino effect.

Each year Gran celebrated Spoleto with a large luncheon in the garden. Although the azaleas, daffodils, and other spring blooms are past, the oppressive heat of the summer is not yet at its peak, and the shady garden provides an oasis-like setting at mid-day.

Yesterday, as I told you, was a gorgeous day. The luncheon ended up sixteen, so I used the two marbleized table tops. Everyone seemed to enjoy it, and the food was light and delicious. After the luncheon there was a party up the street, then I had a quiet hour and off to the North Carolina ballet— marvelous, but quite different from the Harlem. The chamber music concerts this year have been superlative!

~ JWS – 5/30/1983

OWLE

Serves 12.

1½	quarts strawberries
	D.O.M. Benedictine
2½	bottles Rhine wine
1	bottle champagne

Wash the strawberries and cut them in half into a deep punch bowl. Mash them slightly. Cover entirely with Benedictine and soak for 3 hours in a warm place. Add a large block of ice, then mix in the Rhine wine (White Riesling, Johannisburg Riesling, or California Rhine wine) and the champagne. This may also be made with ripe white peaches in season.

ALTED PECANS

Gran ordered her holiday pecans from the orchard in Georgia each fall. They really are larger and fresher than anything you can find in the store. They are delicious with cocktails before dinner when prepared this way, and can also be chopped (unsalted) and used in Pecan Tea Cakes.

3	cups large pecan halves
3	tablespoons olive oil
	Salt

Preheat the oven to 350°. Put the pecans in a single layer in a jelly-roll pan and heat for 15 minutes. Remove pecans from oven and drizzle the olive oil over them. Mix well. Put back in the oven for 10 minutes more. Remove and turn out onto layers of paper towel on top of several layers of newspaper. Salt at once while they are still hot. Cool and store in an airtight tin.

Charleston Shrimp

Serves 8.

¼	pound butter or 8 tablespoons pure olive oil
3	pounds raw shrimp in shell
2	cloves garlic, minced
¼	cup finely chopped celery
½	cup finely chopped onion
½	cup sliced mushrooms
½	cup finely diced red and green bell peppers (optional)
2	teaspoons paprika
2	tablespoons tomato paste
½	teaspoon Tabasco sauce
6	tablespoons flour
2	cups chicken stock
1	cup sour cream
	Salt and more Tabasco to taste

In a 12-inch sauté pan, melt the butter or heat up the olive oil. Add the shrimp in its shell, and cook until it is blush pink. Cool. Remove the shell and take out the black vein. Put an extra tablespoon of butter in the pan if necessary. Add the garlic, celery, onion, mushrooms, peppers, paprika, tomato paste and Tabasco sauce. Stir in the flour and gradually add the chicken stock. Cook until the mixture thickens, stirring constantly. Blend in the sour cream. Add the shrimp back into the sauce and heat through. You may add more Tabasco and salt to taste. Simmer, but do not boil, 10 to 15 minutes, or until the shrimp is heated through.

Rice Ring

3	cups raw rice
1	tablespoon butter

Butter a 2-quart ring mold and set aside. Prepare rice as you usually do. I like Charleston steamed rice as it is sticky and holds together well in the ring. Allow the cooked rice to cool just slightly, then pack it into the buttered ring mold while still warm. If necessary, set the mold in a moderate oven for 5 minutes before unmolding. Unmold rice onto a platter and fill with Charleston Shrimp.

BUTTERED SPINACH

Serves 8.

This is a richly flavored spinach which is excellent as a side dish when you don't want a cream sauce.

2   pounds fresh spinach

2   tablespoons butter

     Salt to taste

¼   teaspoon nutmeg

Cut the tough stems off the spinach leaves and rinse the leaves several times. Bring a large pot of water to a rapid boil, add the spinach and simmer until tender—about 10 minutes. Drain the spinach well, pressing the water out. Chop the spinach as finely as you wish, and season it with the butter, salt and nutmeg.

ORANGE LAYER CAKE

ORANGE CAKE

½	pound butter, softened
2	cups granulated sugar
6	eggs, separated
2	cups cake flour
1	teaspoon baking powder
¼	teaspoon salt
1	cup strained fresh orange juice
2	tablespoons finely grated orange rind

Preheat the oven to 375°. Grease and flour 2 (9-inch) layer pans. Cream the butter. Add sugar and mix well. Beat the egg yolks lightly and add to butter mixture, mixing well. Sift the cake flour with the baking powder and salt, and add it alternately with the orange juice and orange zest. Beat 4 egg whites until they are stiff, but not dry, saving the remaining 2 whites for the icing. Fold the egg whites into the batter. Pour batter into prepared pans and bake for about 30 to 35 minutes or until they test done. Ice with Orange Seven Minute Icing.

ORANGE SEVEN MINUTE ICING

Makes enough to ice a 2-layer cake.

2   egg whites at room temperature
     (reserved from cake)

1½   cups granulated sugar

3   tablespoons strained fresh orange juice

1   teaspoon finely grated orange rind

Put the egg whites, sugar, and orange juice and zest into the top of a double boiler. Beat with an electric beater until it is well mixed. Place over rapidly boiling water, beating constantly, and cook for 7 minutes, or until the icing will stand in peaks. Remove from the heat and continue beating until it is thick enough to spread.

A variation of this refreshing cake is an Orange-Coconut Cake. Add ½ cup grated coconut to the cake batter before folding in the egg whites. Ice the cake with Orange Seven Minute Icing and sprinkle the top with 1 cup grated coconut.

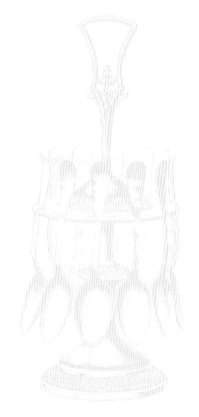

CHAPTER XVII
JULY

A Summer Supper in the Mountains

SAUTÉED MOUNTAIN TROUT

SALAD OF RED AND YELLOW MOUNTAIN TOMATOES

SWEDISH CUCUMBER SALAD

CORN STICKS

STRAWBERRY SHORTCAKE

BLUEBERRY PIE

---

*W*hile many Charleston houses were originally built and occupied by planters who moved to town during the summer to escape the threat of malaria on their plantations, later Charlestonians have traditionally left the city during the hot, sticky summer months. Small wonder, since it is not unusual to have long stretches of days approaching 90 & 90—90 degrees and 90 percent humidity—starting in June and lingering often well into early October.

When my grandparents moved to Charleston in 1942, it was long before air conditioning became commonly used. Of course, in those days, banks and offices closed in early afternoon for dinner; even the schools were dismissed, so that children could join their families for the ritual of the midday meal. In her novel *Three O'Clock Dinner*, published in 1945, Charleston author Josephine Pinckney writes of one of her old Charlestonian characters that he was "ready to compromise with modernity and have the midday meal at two o'clock, but while Etta acknowledged his masculine right to set the hour, she invariably added, 'In Papa's time we dined at three.'" In any case, by the time I moved to Charleston in 1976, the traditional midday dinner hour had been moved from three o'clock to two, and many businesses and schools still closed.

Gran used to recall that in the heat of summer the Broad Street offices closed up by four. People loaded into their cars and headed to Folly Beach or Sullivan's Island to catch the late-afternoon cool breezes and take a dip in the ocean.

Throughout my grandmother's tenure at the house, we had no central air conditioning, although there were window units in certain of the bedrooms and attic fans on the third floor. Windows were left open, especially onto the piazzas, assuring the circulation of air throughout the house during those sultry months. My mother remembers that when they first moved to Charleston in the

The outside porch with its view of the pond provides the perfect setting for a supper of mountain trout and produce followed by a pie brimming with local blueberries.

1940s, the beds were moved to the center of the room and draped with mosquito netting during the heat of the summer.

Until the end of her life, my grandmother continued the tradition of "putting the house away for the summer." This involved rolling up all the carpets, taking down the window hangings, covering all the furniture with slipcovers, and removing pastel and watercolor paintings to the one air-conditioned bedroom so they wouldn't mildew under the glass.

In *Mellowed By Time*, Elizabeth O'Neill Verner describes techniques that Charlestonians deployed to survive the long, hot, sultry summer:

> We strip our houses of all unnecessary draperies, install cool matting rugs and electric fans... the city thins out; one by one the houses are closed. Off most of us go to the beaches and the mountains.
>
> The old city sleeps. The few that stay at home know how to take it. The heavy shutters are hooked in to keep out the glare and heat. Shopping is done early, or late in the afternoon; no one hurries. There are no sunstrokes; the gentle breezes from the sea bring relief, and when it all seems too unbearable, a blessed roll of thunder is heard. Quick vivid zigzags of lightning follow and a tropical storm brings respite for awhile.

In her later years we tried to convince Gran to install air conditioning so that she wouldn't have to go through so much work at the beginning and end of each summer. But her response was that even with air conditioning, she would still feel she needed to "put the house away." I know how much work this entails, as

I did it for many years until the central air conditioning for the whole house was completed in 2001. Still, like Gran, I must admit that when the wide pine floors are completely bare, the dark silk and scratchy needlework covered in light cotton, and the exterior shutters pulled shut on the front, the whole house feels cooler.

Since the 1800s, Charlestonians have closed up their houses in summer and retreated to one of the numerous nearby beaches or to the North Carolina mountains to escape the oppressive heat. Just a four-to-six-hour drive from Charleston, the mountain locales—such as Asheville, Brevard, Cashiers, and Highlands—offer majestic beauty, superb opportunities to fish and hike, and temperatures that average ten to fifteen degrees cooler than those of Charleston.

In my grandparents' case, they had kept a summer home in Connecticut for many years after moving to Charleston. But as they got older, the long seasonal trip became increasingly difficult. My grandfather fondly remembered his summers spent in the Berkshire Mountains of western Massachusetts; he loved that rolling green terrain. A longtime friend suggested he look at western North Carolina, saying "I think it will remind you a lot of the Berkshires." It did; and in 1962, we spent our first summer at Cherokee Trace, named for the old Indian trail or "trace" that ran through the property. The property itself consisted of eighteen wooded acres with a stream running through it, a pond full of trout, and mountain trails. My grandfather designed and built a house there, which he and my grandmother enjoyed together for many years. The house and grounds remain in our family to this day.

Cherokee Trace was a magical place for us as children. In June, my parents would drive us from Ohio to North Carolina, where we were left with my grandparents for the entire glorious summer. My brothers hiked and fished, and later helped maintain the hiking trails for the local inn. I spent my days at the nearby riding camp, riding and helping care for the horses—and feeling

like I'd died and gone to heaven. Somewhere in the midst of these long stretches with my grandparents, I began first to observe my grandmother cooking, and later to learn by her side.

I remember well the dinners of local brook or rainbow trout sautéed in butter and lemon. At that time, the small pond—which we shared with about five other houses—was well stocked. My grandfather had bamboo poles for us children, which we baited with worms. He used his fly rod. We all loved to fish with him, although my brother Phil couldn't stand to see his fish served up at the table. So Gran always served him a meat pattie—which he ate alone on the outside porch while we enjoyed the fresh trout indoors.

In the mornings my grandfather—who was an early riser—often made his special popovers; they would be waiting for us when we came downstairs. Sunday noon dinners were a special treat...except for those times when Gran served tongue. I well remember her rolling out the warming cart into the dining room. There, on a platter, would be the entire grey, bumpy tongue which, unfortunately, looked exactly like what it was! (I have not included that particular recipe.) But even the tongue was more than made up for by whatever dessert happened to be that day: a pie brimming with our own hand-picked blueberries; homemade shortcake biscuits oozing with our glistening red raspberries; or slices of local peaches, topped with whipped cream.

The berry patch was one of the highlights of the summer. On a trip to England, my grandparents had seen a "berry room"—a berry garden enclosed by four walls and a roof made of chicken wire. This chicken-wire architecture made it impossible for the birds to get in, and left the bushes drooping with berries for the picking. My grandparents built their own berry room in the mountains, and filled it with raspberry and blueberry bushes; these bore quantities of fruit throughout the summer. We feasted on blueberry pies and raspberry shortcake, supplemented by the fragrant peaches we could buy from just down the mountain in South Carolina. For a number of years we also had a marvelous cherry tree just outside the kitchen, which produced the juicy sour cherries so delicious in pie or preserves.

In addition to growing our own fruits, we shopped daily at Fowler's market in town. The Fowlers, a local family, grew fruits and vegetables to sell: their own delicious berries; tender local mountain lettuces; succulent red and yellow tomatoes. For years, we also bought loaves of the most wonderful toasting bread I have ever had. It was made by a local woman named Mildred. We bought loaves of Mildred's bread daily throughout the summer; at the end of the season, we brought a dozen or so loaves home to be put in the freezer.

While Mildred's recipe sadly seems to have been lost at her death, I have included here a recipe for English Muffin Bread which is a not-dissimilar dense bread, delicious toasted. If you're going to have good toast, you must have great jam to put on it—not too thick or rubbery, not too sweet, and with an abundant flavor of the fruit. In our later years in the mountains—when I returned with my own children in the summers—jam making was a priority. On any given afternoon, you could catch Gran in the kitchen, wearing her long, flower-printed apron—her reading glasses hanging around her neck—stirring a pot of jam. Just let her hear in the morning that the Fowlers had fresh raspberries, and there would be a jam-making afternoon sure to follow. Quantities of peach, raspberry, blackberry, and strawberry jams (along with numerous loaves of Mildred's bread) would have to be squeezed into the car at the end of the summer for the trip back to Charleston, where they would be served to family and house guests throughout the winter months.

There are two things that make these old-fashioned preserving recipes better than any others. First, the jam is cooked in small batches without any artificial pectin. It thickens due to the natural pectin in the fruit itself; I find the flavor is much more intense than in preserves made with pectin added. Moreover, the lack of added pectin makes for what I find is a much nicer consistency—it's never too thick or rubbery. Second, the recipes call for less sugar than many recipes; again, I find this means the true flavor of the fruit is enhanced rather than masked by being over-sweetened. The closest I have found to these recipes are the artisanal preserves one can buy in Europe.

I still try to make lots of jam during the summer and put it up in half-pint jars. If you can keep the family from eating it all, these make wonderful gifts at Christmas. I start in the spring when the local Wadmalaw Island strawberries are ripe, and try to get flavorful local fruits throughout the summer at our weekly farmers market. I also never miss an opportunity to buy a basket of superb South Carolina peaches from the orchard I pass on my way to the mountains of North Carolina.

This mountain menu makes the most of the mountain produce and fresh local trout. I serve it with what I consider real southern cornbread—thin, golden, and, preferably, baked in a cast iron skillet. To my way of thinking, any cornbread made with flour or sugar is Yankee cornbread!

I don't know when I have enjoyed the mountains more. The house and grounds were all in such perfect order, and have never looked better, in spite of much rainy weather. I missed the Frog and Owl [restaurant] *and the blackberries, but loved seeing the young people, and you and Robert* [my father] *were wonderful with all of them, providing all of them with a store of happy memories. More and more in this period, it is a special thing to be able to step off the fast track now and then and re-charge.*

~ JWS – 8/2/85

Sautéed Mountain Trout

Serves 4.

This is the absolute best way to serve fresh trout—brook trout, rainbow trout or brown trout—whether you catch it yourself or carry it home from the store!

4	fresh trout, cleaned
¼	cup butter
1	lemon
	Parsley

Melt butter in a large sauté pan with the juice of the lemon. Add fish and sauté until they are firm to the touch. Remove to a platter and garnish with chopped parsley.

Swedish Cucumber Salad

Serves 4.

2	cups thinly sliced cucumbers
1	tablespoon salt
¼	cup white wine vinegar
1	tablespoon sugar
	Freshly ground pepper
	Parsley or dill, chopped

Peel the cucumbers and slice paper thin (this is easiest in the food processor). Put the slices in a bowl and sprinkle with the salt. Mix well. Place a plate on top of the cucumbers and weight it down. Let stand 2 hours, then drain off the liquid and rinse thoroughly. The cucumbers will retain a salty flavor, but make sure any excess is rinsed off. Mix the vinegar, sugar and pepper and toss with the cucumber slices. Stir in the parsley or dill, and chill several hours.

These cucumbers are very pungent. So it is best to store them in a container with a tight-fitting lid.

Corn Sticks

2	tablespoons vegetable shortening
2	cups cornmeal
2	teaspoons baking powder
1	teaspoon baking soda
1	teaspoon salt
1	egg
1	cup buttermilk

Preheat oven to 400°. Divide the vegetable shortening between two 6-stick cast iron corn stick pans. Place the pans in the preheated oven until the shortening is melted and the pans are hot. Meanwhile, stir together the cornmeal, baking powder, baking soda and salt. Lightly beat the egg and add it along with the buttermilk to the cornmeal mixture, blending gently. Remove the pans from the oven and pour in the batter, filling each mold about ⅔ full. Bake for 15 minutes.

You can also bake this as a thin crisp cornbread using a 10-inch cast iron pan. In that case, bake the cornbread for 25 to 35 minutes, or until golden.

Blueberry Pie

4	cups blueberries
	Lemon juice
1	cup sugar
⅛	teaspoon salt
2	tablespoons flour
¼	teaspoon cinnamon
	Dash of nutmeg
1-2	tablespoons butter

Preheat oven to 450°. Wash blueberries and dry them on paper towels. Put them in a large bowl and sprinkle with lemon juice. In a small bowl, mix the sugar, salt, flour, cinnamon, and nutmeg. Stir it into the blueberries and distribute well. Line a 9- or 10-inch pie plate with Flakey Pie Crust (see page 176). Add the berries, and dot with butter. Top with remaining crust and cut small vents in the top. Set pie on cookie sheet and bake for 10 minutes at 450°, then reduce temperature to 350° and bake for 25 to 35 minutes longer, or until the filling is bubbling through the vents. Serve at room temperature.

STRAWBERRY SHORTCAKE

8 to 10 (3-inch) biscuits.

In the summers we often made shortcake with raspberries or ripe South Carolina peaches—equally delicious!

SHORTCAKE BISCUITS

2	cups all-purpose flour
4	teaspoons baking powder
½	teaspoon salt
2	teaspoons sugar
2	tablespoons butter
1	tablespoon vegetable shortening
⅔	cup whole milk

Preheat the oven to 450°. Sift the flour with the baking powder, salt and sugar. Cut in the butter and vegetable shortening with a pastry blender until it has the consistency of coarse cornmeal. Gradually add the milk and stir until the dough pulls together into a ball. Roll the dough out on a floured surface to a thickness of about ½-inch. Cut into 3-inch rounds and place on an ungreased cookie sheet. Bake in the upper third of the oven for 10 to 12 minutes.

STRAWBERRY SAUCE

1	quart ripe strawberries
¼-½	cup granulated sugar

Wash and de-stem the strawberries, and halve them if they are large. Add the sugar—you may add more or less to taste and depending on the ripeness of the berries. Mash the berries slightly with a potato masher and let them macerate until the juice runs out. To serve, split the cooled shortcake biscuits in halve. Fill and top with the strawberries, and add a dollop of sweetened or unsweetened whipped cream according to your taste.

> *The climate is marvelous after the heat of Charleston. To have put on a sweater last night, and have the heat on for a short period—it is incredible, all within a five-hour trip.*
>
> ~ JWS – 7/16/72

Epilogue

After decades of travel to various regions of France, my grandmother finally returned to the southern provinces in 1984. Arriving in Nice, she and my mother rented a car and toured the Côte d'Azur and the hill towns behind it. Gran marveled at the drive along the Gorge du Loup, the steep winding road that switches back and forth along the cliffs between Cannes and Monte Carlo. She remembered her travels sixty years earlier when it was merely a gravel road, later writing wistfully, "Every time I go to France I experience something new as well as renew impressions of well loved old friends."

One of her memories of her year as a young woman in Antibes was of a villa she passed frequently which bore a faience plaque that read *La Maison de Grand-mère*—Grandmother's House. After she was widowed, she bought a small house in Charleston directly across the street from hers. It served for many years as a guest house for Gran and later, for a time, as my home when my children were young. When Gran became ill in 1988, she moved to this smaller house. It provided her with the convenience of a bed and bath on the first floor throughout her final years. One year on a trip to France, Mother and I ordered a plaque from the famous French ceramic works at Quimper; that sign—*La Maison de Grand-mère*—hung next to the front gate at the little house for many years.

In 2003, my mother and I visited my daughter who was studying in Paris. The three of us made a trip together to the south of France. Mother wondered why, in all the previous trips to France, my grandmother had never suggested that we search for the villa in Antibes or drive by the old casino in Juan-les-Pins. I like to think that she preferred to preserve them in her memory as they were in the 1920s—and as they appear to me in the old black-and-white photos. But in 2003 (more than a decade after her death), the three of us—armed with old names, references, and photographs—resolved to track down the *Villa Champ Tercier* in the hills above Antibes. As we rounded a bend, Mother gasped "There it is!" Partially concealed by its high wall and garden (grown tall and lush over many decades), the house was nevertheless recognizable from my grandmother's photos. Writing a hasty note explaining our long-ago connection to the property, we slipped it, along with copies of old family photographs, through the mail slot in the gate. We soon heard back from the gracious French family who had moved in only the week before. Inviting us to visit, they told us that the now-renamed villa had just undergone a complete renovation. That is how three generations of women came to enjoy having tea in the same spot overlooking the azure Mediterranean as had two generations of family members seventy-seven years before.

In the late 1990s, I traveled to France with a close friend from Charleston who had known my grandmother. While my friend had been to France a number of times, it was her first visit to the Côte d'Azur and Provence. As we strolled through the cobbled streets of one of the many hillside villages, we marveled at the warm ochres and soft creamy yellows of the walls and the weathered blues and greens of the doors and shutters. My friend asked, "Do you think your grandmother chose the colors for her house in Charleston from the colors she remembered in the south of France?" I had never before made that connection, but indeed I am sure that my grandparents—who, after all, met in the south of France—rekindled those memories when they first visited Charleston. The brilliant sunlight of the Lowcountry and the pastel walls of the buildings—shabbier and far less pristine than they are in the affluent Charleston of today, but arguably more endearing—surely brought to mind those days in the *Villa Champ Tercier*.

Her year in France sparked a lifelong love of that country, which she passed on to my mother and to two more generations; it seemed to wind like a thread through the rest of her life, infusing her travels and her entertaining. In 1959, she had the occasion to entertain the French ambassador and his wife during their visit to Charleston. My mother recalls that we were vacationing in Charleston at the time, and she was included in the dinner. She relates that after the meal—as they were enjoying conversation and after-dinner drinks in the drawing room—I, age six, was allowed to appear briefly in my pajamas to meet the ambassador. By all accounts, he was charmed.

As I look back at the parties I attended and those I read about in her letters and diaries, I realize that Gran's gift was her ability to relate to anyone—from the French ambassador to the country neighbor. She was fascinated by people from all walks of life and eager to hear their thoughts and views of the world. Her extensive reading and travels meant that she was conversant on any topic from finance to porcelains to the history of China. In turn, her interest in what her guests had to say made each of them feel like the most important person in the world at that moment—surely the hallmark of a good hostess.

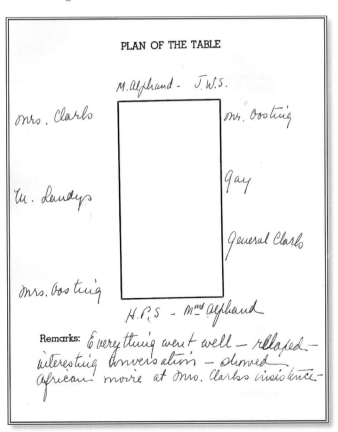

Where given at home - Charleston   Date March 21 1959

Occasion

Guests Present
Hervé Alphand - Ambassador of France -
M.me Alphand
M. Pierre Landys - aide -
General Mark Clark
Mrs. Mark Clark
Mr. Oosting
Mrs. Oosting
Gay Staats Huffman

Menu
Shrimp Consommé
Veal Scallopine with mushrooms -
Rice
Green beans
Caramel pecan roll
Caramel sauce
Demi-Tasse

Unable to Attend

Wines
Chambertin 1949
Cave de l'Hotel de la Côte d'or -

Table Decorations Elaborate linen cloth - lace center + insets to
Pinks, rose + white camellias in low center dish + two
small purple glass bowls - silver candlesticks - purple cased glass
etc - etc -

PLAN OF THE TABLE

M. Alphand - J.W.S.

Mrs. Clark   Mr. Oosting

M. Landys   Gay

                             General Clark

Mrs. Oosting

H.P.S - M.me Alphand

Remarks: Everything went well - relaxed -
interesting conversation - showed
African movie at Mrs. Clarks insistence -

133

Gran continued entertaining into her eighties, still enjoying time in the kitchen to prepare the many dishes for which she had become well known in Charleston. Whether it was a luncheon or supper party for six or for thirty, she continued to prepare much of the meal, to arrange the flowers, and to charm her guests of all generations. When giving parties for my age group in the 1970s and 80s, she professed surprise that our friends wanted her to participate as a guest and not just be relegated to the kitchen. Indeed, my friends were as fascinated by her as she was by them; they were especially delighted to be seated at her table.

As a friend recently suggested, entertaining was Gran's art form. It allowed her to weave her talents and interests together: cooking; flower arranging; creating an artful setting using her beloved house, garden, and pieces from her collections; assembling lively mixes of people; and stimulating conversation and thought. Certainly she was a product of her time, but I harbor the hope that her art form is not one that is lost to us in the modern age.

Gran was widowed in 1971 at the relatively young age of sixty-five. In a quiet summer in the mountains six months later, she reflected on what she wanted the rest of her life to be:

....to travel, to read much more, to have the great gift of time, to even take some course I would like to audit. Not to let the majority of people I see be my age or older. I need and want fresh ideas, fresh insight, even when I may not agree. I am a people person, and I enjoy seeing and being with people. I enjoy a certain amount of social life, even if my definition of that phrase is long-gone into the past. I will admit that I live in the only small island where any remnant of that way of life exists, and believe me it is changing from day to day even there. People are giving up one way after another, old ways of living, and perhaps along with it, old ways of thinking. And it is not all bad.

As I look at Charleston today, I wonder if it is still that "small island" where a traditional way of life and entertaining continues to exist. Although the numbers of tourists who visit today—not just seasonally but throughout all twelve months—seem to threaten, at times, to sink the peninsula, we enjoy vibrancy here—in our shops, restaurants and arts scene—that far exceeds any vision my grandparents could have had for Charleston when they first encountered it sixty-five years ago. Their beloved eighteenth- and nineteenth-century buildings, many of which once teetered on the verge of falling down, are now restored—gleaming and glossy, albeit often empty while their owners live elsewhere most of the year. The sight of nannies pushing babies to the park for a morning outing, or mothers escorting toddlers up the sidewalk to nursery school, is, sadly, a rarity. Most often those young families can no longer afford to live in the houses where they grew up, and have moved to newer communities across one of two rivers—the Ashley or Cooper—that bound the old city. Our City Market now caters almost exclusively to tourists. The picturesque marketplace where locals once could buy jewel-like okra and squash has morphed into a lively tourist bazaar where souvenirs, trinkets, and local crafts are sold. And the pressures of a rapidly expanding urban center—pushing outward at a staggering rate each year—threaten the forests, waterways, and farms that have defined the Lowcountry for so long.

Yet the winter season continues to bring oyster roasts at country plantations. The debutantes are feted throughout the season at a myriad of balls, luncheons, and teas. The ladies still arrive decked out in their best gowns, jewels, and furs. Downtown residents still entertain at home, albeit mostly at parties and events where caterers—rather than the ladies of the house—provide the food. And there are cold, clear evenings when I walk along the dark sidewalks, savoring the fragrance of wood smoke drifting from nearby chimneys; when I can almost forget how much the city has changed; when a glimpse, a sound, or smell can have me believing that this is still the sleepy, slightly shabby town of decades ago.

Then I remember that even Gran—who lived in a time of staggering changes, who moved from a childhood of baking in wood-burning ovens and hitching the team to a wagon when it was time to shop for supplies to an adulthood of witnessing space travel and the development of mind-boggling technology—marveled and wondered at the inventions, changes, and new ideas that emerged throughout her eight decades. I acknowledge that those changes are sometimes bittersweet, and I often long for that simpler and slower time when to visit Charleston was to step into a rarefied world of gentility, tranquility, and grace. I recognize that, even here, people are giving up old ways of living and old ways of thinking. And, like Gran, I remind myself that it is not all bad.

Three generations ~ 1963

Drinks

Iced Brazilian Chocolate

Serves 4 to 6.

1   cup strong hot coffee
2   ounces unsweetened chocolate
4   tablespoons sugar
4   cups whole milk, scalded

Melt the chocolate over hot water and combine with the sugar. Add coffee gradually, stirring constantly. Add the scalded milk and cook for 10 minutes until the mixture is smooth, stirring constantly. Chill and serve with spoonfuls of ice cream in a glass, or top with whipped cream.

Soups

Fresh Mushroom Soup

1   pound mushrooms
3   tablespoons butter
1   rounded tablespoon flour
2   cups whole milk
    Salt to taste

Clean and trim the mushrooms, saving some of the stems. Grind the mushrooms in a food processor, leaving them as chunky as you wish. Put in a medium saucepan with the butter, and heat thoroughly. Add the flour, and cook for 2 minutes. Slowly stir in the cold milk. Cook 5 minutes, then put in a double boiler and let simmer for 1 hour before serving. Add salt last.

The first part of the soup can be made ahead until the final hour of cooking.

Turkey Soup

This is a great way to use up the leftover Thanksgiving turkey. We often serve it for Christmas Eve supper along with a green salad and Aunt Matina's Greek Holiday Bread. It freezes perfectly.

1	turkey carcass, cooked
1	bunch celery
1	pound carrots
2	onions
1	bunch parsley
⅔	cup rice
	Salt and pepper to taste

Put the leftover turkey carcass in a 16-quart stockpot. You may have to pull off legs and wings to make it fit. Fill the pot with cold water until it covers the turkey. Break in half 2 stalks celery with the leaves on, and add to the pot. Add two carrots, unpeeled and broken roughly. Cut 1 onion, skin on, in quarters and add it to the pot. Add several sprigs of parsley, whole. Bring to a boil over high heat, then turn the heat down and simmer for 1 to 1½ hours, covered. Check to make sure the meat is coming off the bone. Cool and strain into bowls. (You will have several quarts of broth, so you'll need a big stockpot and large bowls.) Chill the broth several hours or overnight. When the turkey is cool enough to handle, pick all the good meat off the bones and reserve. Put broth back in your kettle. Add the turkey meat. Peel and slice the remaining carrots. Chop the remaining celery and peel, halve, and slice thinly the remaining onion. Add the vegetables along with ¼ cup finely chopped parsley to the pot along with the rice. Bring to a boil and simmer for 1 hour, or until rice is cooked.

Salads and Dressings

Salad with Italian Dressing

Serves 6 moderate portions. Double this for 8 or 10 good salad eaters.

This salad is really special, and is best made with Boston or other soft lettuce.

Italian Dressing

4	eggs
1	teaspoon salt
½	teaspoon freshly ground pepper
1	teaspoon sugar
½	teaspoon paprika
1	teaspoon dry mustard
2	tablespoons cream
1	tablespoon Worcestershire sauce
2	tablespoons white wine tarragon vinegar
1	teaspoon onion juice
4	tablespoons olive oil

Hard-boil the eggs, and cut out the yolks. Reserve egg whites for the salad. Rice or mash the yolks with a fork, and mix them with the dry ingredients. Gradually add the liquids and vinegar, adding the olive oil last, and blend well.

For the Salad

1	clove garlic
1	can anchovies
1	head Boston lettuce, or other soft variety
4	hard-boiled egg whites, reserved from dressing

Rub your salad bowl with the cut clove of garlic. Break the lettuce into pieces, and add the anchovies which have been drained and cut into pieces. Mix the salad well with the dressing. Rice the egg whites over the top.

CHUTNEY DRESSING

This is especially delicious on Belgian endive.

½	teaspoon salt
¼	teaspoon paprika
½	teaspoon dry mustard
½	cup olive oil
2	tablespoons white wine vinegar
2	heaping tablespoons chutney, finely chopped

Mix dry ingredients. Add oil and vinegar and chutney. Correct seasonings to taste.

Soufflés and Casseroles

Make-Ahead Cheese Soufflé

Serves 4 to 6.

8	thin slices day-old white bread
4	tablespoons butter, softened
1	pound sharp Cheddar, grated
6	eggs, slightly beaten
1½	cups half & half
1	cup whole milk
1	rounded teaspoon light brown sugar
¼	teaspoon paprika
1	green onion, finely minced (or 1 tablespoon grated onion)
½	teaspoon dry mustard
½	teaspoon salt
¼	teaspoon coarsely ground black pepper
1	teaspoon Worcestershire sauce
⅛	teaspoon cayenne pepper

Cut the crusts off the bread. Butter it and dice it into squares about ¼ inch. Butter a 3-quart casserole dish. Arrange half of the diced bread on the bottom of the casserole. Cover with half the grated cheese. Add the remaining bread, then the remaining cheese. Whisk together the eggs, half & half and milk with the seasonings. Pour the mixture over the bread and cheese. This should all be done the day before serving up to this point. Cover the casserole and refrigerate overnight. The next day, remove the casserole from the refrigerator and preheat the oven to 300°. Uncover the dish and set in a shallow pan large enough to hold it. Pour hot water about 1 inch up the side of the casserole. Bake on the middle rack of the oven for 1 hour 20 minutes. Check after 1 hour. If it is getting too browned, you can cover the dish with a piece of foil for the final 20 minutes.

This is a very easy dish that can be made up to 2 to 3 days before serving. Unlike a real soufflé, it can wait for up to 20 minutes if you need time before serving. Just turn the oven off and let the casserole stand in it. For a delicious variation, you may also add 1 pound of crabmeat divided between the bread and cheese layers. Serve with a simple green salad and crusty bread.

BAKED SPAGHETTI CASSEROLE

This was one of our favorite family suppers when we were young. It is still a favorite of the next generation. It can be prepared completely in advance and refrigerated. If you do so, allow longer for it to bake.

4-6	slices bacon
½	pound ground beef
1	(28-ounce) can Italian tomatoes with juice
¼	cup diced onion
½	teaspoon salt
¼	teaspoon coarsely ground black pepper
2	teaspoons sugar
2	teaspoons Worcestershire sauce
¼	cup catsup
3	ounces cream cheese
3	ounce can sliced mushrooms (optional)
½	pound spaghetti
¼	pound sharp Cheddar cheese

Preheat oven to 350°. Fry the bacon until fairly crisp and set aside. In the same pan, brown the ground beef. In another large pan, mix the tomatoes (cut up if you like) with their juice, and the seasonings. Break the cream cheese into chunks, and add it to the tomato sauce, stirring it in well. Meanwhile, boil spaghetti according to package directions and drain. Mix the beef and tomato sauce together. Pour sauce over drained spaghetti, mixing well. Put the mixture into a shallow casserole and top with slices of Cheddar cheese to cover. Bake until hot, about 30 minutes if you're cooking it immediately off the stove. Add the strips of bacon over the top for the last 10 minutes or so of baking.

Staats Chicken Casserole for a Crowd

Serves 20.

20 boneless, skinless chicken breast halves

½ cup all-purpose flour

Salt and pepper for seasoning flour

¼ cup olive oil

2 tablespoons butter

½ onion, chopped

1½ pounds mushrooms

½ lemon

1½ quarts (6 cups) chopped fresh or canned tomatoes

3 cups chicken broth

½ teaspoon saffron

½ cup dry white wine

3 cups rice

1½ (10-ounce) packages frozen peas

1½ (10-ounce) packages frozen artichoke hearts

Strips of pimento

Chopped parsley

Preheat the oven to 300°. Dust the chicken breasts with the seasoned flour, and brown in a large skillet in some of the olive oil and the butter. Remove the chicken pieces to a large shallow casserole. If you don't have a large enough dish, you may assemble it in a roasting pan. Next add more oil to the pan if needed, and cook the chopped onion until soft and transparent. Add the mushrooms which have been cleaned and quartered. Stir in the juice of the lemon half, and continue cooking until the juice is extracted from the mushrooms, about 10 minutes. Add to the mushrooms the chopped tomatoes with their juice. While you're preparing the mushrooms, put 1 cup of the chicken broth in a saucepan, and add the saffron, allowing it to soak. Add the remaining broth and bring it all to a boil. Turn off the heat and add the white wine. Arrange the chicken breasts so there is just one layer in the casserole, setting the rest aside for the moment. Over the layers of chicken, scatter the uncooked rice and peas alternately with the tomato and mushroom mixture, adding back in the additional layers of chicken breast and layering with the vegetables. Pour the broth and wine mixture over all. Cover the casserole and cook for 1 to 1½ hours or until the rice is tender. In the skillet, add additional olive oil and cook the artichoke hearts until tender. When you are ready to serve, garnish the dish with the hot artichoke hearts, strips of pimento and lots of chopped parsley.

This may be partially prepared a day in advance. Brown the chicken breasts, prepare the tomato/mushroom mixture and assemble. The next day, stir the rice and peas through the chicken and pour over it the broth mixture. If you wish you may also add small shrimp cooked in butter or olive oil as an additional garnish before serving. Serve with a good green salad and a Virginia ham for a complete meal.

CHICKEN AND RED WINE CASSEROLE

Serves 4.

1	clove garlic
2	tablespoons olive oil
1	3-4 pound chicken, cut into quarters
½	cup condensed tomato soup
1½	cups red wine
2	tomatoes, peeled and quartered
1	stalk celery, diced
3	large potatoes, peeled and diced
2	shallots, minced
2	leeks, chopped (or substitute 1 bunch green onions for the shallots and leek)
½	cup green peas
	Salt and pepper to taste

Preheat oven to 350°. In a large skillet, add the garlic to the olive oil, then add the chicken pieces and sauté until brown. Remove the chicken to a casserole large enough to hold all the ingredients. Add the tomato soup, wine, and vegetables to the pan. Stir and heat through. Add salt and pepper to taste. Pour the mixture over the chicken pieces, and bake for 1 hour.

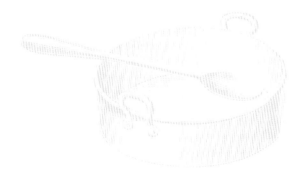

Meats

Chicken Hash

Serves 4.

3   tablespoons butter
3   tablespoons flour
1½   cups chicken broth
½   cup whole milk
½   teaspoon salt
¼   teaspoon mace
¼   teaspoon black pepper
     Grated rind of ½ lemon
3   cups diced cooked chicken

In a heavy saucepan large enough to hold all of the ingredients, melt the butter. Add the flour and cook for 2 minutes. Slowly add the chicken broth and milk, stirring constantly. Add the seasonings, and continue cooking until the sauce is thick. Add the chicken and heat thoroughly.

This is a good way to use up left over chicken. Serve with crisp bacon curls or small sausages. You may add 2 tablespoons dry sherry to the sauce. Sprinkle with ½ cup grated Parmesan and heat under the broiler until brown and bubbly.

MARINATED LEG OF LAMB

Serves about 8.

½   cup olive oil

2   teaspoons salt

1   teaspoon black pepper

    Juice of 2 large lemons

1   clove garlic, minced

    A "healthy infusion" of thyme, parsley and
      oregano chopped (fresh if possible)

2   onions, sliced or chopped

1   bay leaf

2   cups wine (either red or white according to
      your preference)

1   leg of lamb, about 5 to 7 pounds

Mix all the ingredients together and marinate a small leg of lamb in the mixture for 24 hours, turning it several times. Roast the lamb at 350° for 1¼ to 1½ hours or according to your taste, basting with the strained marinade. Check the temperature with an instant-read thermometer, 130° for rosy rare or 140° for medium.

MOM'S BEEF STEW

Serves 6 to 8.

This is my Mom's wonderful meaty recipe for beef stew. You can add any other vegetables you wish.

4	tablespoons butter
⅓	cup chopped onion
½	cup flour
3	pounds beef stew meat
1	pound carrots, peeled and sliced
1	(10-ounce) can beef consommé
1	(6-ounce) can tomato paste
	Diced potatoes or other vegetables if you like

Preheat the oven to 350°. Melt the butter in a large skillet. Add the onion and cook until translucent. Dredge the meat in the flour and add to the pan, browning it in the butter. Remove the beef and onion to a casserole. Add the tomato paste to the pan and gradually add the consommé, stirring until smooth. Pour over the meat. Stir in the carrot slices and any other vegetables you want to add. Add a bit of water if the sauce seems too thick. Bake in the oven for 2 hours.

MOM'S MEAT LOAF

Serves 6 to 8.

When I was a child I never understood why people looked down on meat loaf. I loved it, and now it seems to be making a come-back as a comfort food. This makes a big loaf. So I usually freeze half of it.

3	pounds ground beef
1	can tomato soup
1	cup seasoned bread crumbs
1	egg
¼	cup finely chopped onion
1	tablespoon Worcestershire sauce
	Salt and pepper to taste

Preheat the oven to 350°. Mix all ingredients together well. You may do this in a heavy duty mixer or with your hands (although it's a bit goopy!). Shape it into a loaf and set in a roasting pan. Bake for 1 hour.

Game

*Roast Doves*

Serves about 10.

20   wild doves
½   pound butter, softened
      Salt and pepper to taste
1   cup dry white wine
1   cup chicken stock
½   teaspoon thyme
2   bay leaves
1   small onion, halved
2   teaspoons Worcestershire sauce
½   cup chopped parsley

Preheat the oven to 350°. Rub the outside of each dove with softened butter and put a small lump of butter inside the cavity of each bird. Sprinkle each with salt and pepper and put in a large roasting pan. Roast doves about 10 minutes. While they are in the oven, put the wine, chicken stock, thyme, bay leaves, onion and Worcestershire into a sauce pan and bring to a boil. Pour the mixture over the doves and continue roasting them for 1 hour longer, or until they are tender, but not dry. If the sauce is evaporating, put a lid on the roaster for the last 30 minutes. Baste the birds frequently. Sprinkle with chopped parsley before serving.

Roast Venison

Serves 6 to 8.

The first time I cooked venison, one of my friends told me that the only secret was to "marinate the fool out of it." She was right.

2	cups dry red wine
2	cups water
2	large onions
2	teaspoons salt
1	tablespoon peppercorns
3	bay leaves
1	tablespoon whole cloves
1	tablespoon whole allspice
2	tablespoons sugar
2	stalks celery, chopped
2	carrots, sliced
1	venison roast, about 5 pounds
	Several garlic cloves
	Salt pork or bacon
1	cup cream *or* 1 tablespoon cognac
½	cup sour cream
4	ounces currant jelly

Place the meat in a large, deep glass or ceramic container. Mix the wine, water, seasonings, celery, and carrots and pour over the venison. It should come about half way up the roast. Marinate venison in the refrigerator for at least 24 hours and as much as 3 to 4 days, turning it several times. Take the meat out of the marinade and pat it dry. Lard it with salt pork or bacon and insert slivers of garlic. Put in a roasting pan with 1 cup of the marinade. Cover and cook at 325° for 3 hours or so—30 minutes to the pound. Continue to baste the venison and add more marinade as needed. Remove the cover for the last 30 minutes so that it will brown. To finish the sauce, you may add 1 cup of cream or you may add 1 tablespoon cognac, ½ cup sour cream and 4 ounces currant jelly.

Seafood

EASY SHRIMP CASSEROLE

Serves 4.

3   slices white bread

¾   cup whole milk

2   heaping cups chopped cooked shrimp

3   tablespoons butter, melted

2   teaspoons Worcestershire sauce

1   ounce dry sherry

¼   teaspoon nutmeg

     Pinch of mace

     Salt and coarsely ground black pepper to taste

Preheat oven to 350°. Remove the crust from the bread and soak it in the milk in a large bowl, crushing it with a fork. Add the shrimp and seasonings, tossing all together. Put in a buttered casserole and bake for 30 minutes.

CURRIED SHRIMP

Serves 6 to 8.

This is even better made a day ahead and reheated. If you cannot find candied ginger, you may substitute golden raisins.

⅓	cup butter
3	tablespoons flour
1	tablespoon curry powder
½	teaspoon salt
¼	teaspoon paprika
¼	teaspoon nutmeg
2	cups half & half
2	tablespoons finely chopped candied ginger
1	tablespoon lemon juice
1	tablespoon dry sherry
1	tablespoon onion juice
	Dash of Worcestershire sauce
3	cups cooked shrimp

Melt the butter in the top of a double boiler or in a heavy sauce pan. Stir in the flour, curry powder, salt, paprika, and nutmeg. Blend until smooth and cook for 2 minutes. Gradually add the half & half. Stir until it thickens. Add the chopped ginger, lemon juice, sherry and onion juice. Stir in the Worcestershire sauce and add the shrimp. Heat through and serve over rice.

CRABCAKES

Serves 8.

4	slices white bread
½	cup olive oil
⅛	teaspoon dry mustard
½	teaspoon salt
	Dash of paprika
1	teaspoon Worcestershire sauce
2	eggs, separated
1	tablespoon chopped parsley
1	pound crabmeat
1	pound crab claw meat

Trim crusts from bread. Lay the slices in a flat pan or platter and pour olive oil over them. Let stand 1 hour. Pull apart lightly with 2 forks. To the small bits of bread, add seasonings, yolks of eggs and the crabmeat. Mix lightly with a fork. Beat the egg whites until stiff, and fold into the crab mixture. Shape into about 18 small cakes. Brush a hot skillet with olive oil and sauté the crab cakes until brown.

If carefully mixed, these crab cakes will be light and fluffy.

DEVILED CRAB

Serves 4 to 6.

This dish retains all the delicate flavor of the crab.

2	eggs, hard-boiled
¼	teaspoon dried thyme (or 1 teaspoon fresh, minced)
1	tablespoon minced fresh parsley
1	pound fresh crabmeat
	Tabasco sauce or cayenne pepper to taste
	Salt to taste
4	tablespoons butter
¼	cup finely chopped onion
1	cup fresh grated bread crumbs

Preheat oven to 350°. Pick over the crab to make sure there is no shell in it. Chop the hard-boiled eggs and mix with the thyme and parsley. Add to the crabmeat, mixing well. Season highly using Tabasco or cayenne and add salt. Melt two tablespoons of the butter in a large sauté pan and add the chopped onion. Cook until golden and add the crab mixture. Cook about 5 minutes, stirring constantly. Remove from the stove and fill crab shells or small ramekins. Sprinkle lightly with bread crumbs and dot with remaining butter. Bake for about 10 minutes until crab is a delicate brown and thoroughly heated.

CRABMEAT BAKED IN SHELLS

Serves 4 to 6.

7	tablespoons butter
3	tablespoons flour
1½	cups fish or clam broth
2	egg yolks
1	tablespoon lemon juice
	Cayenne pepper to taste
1	pound crabmeat
	Parmesan cheese, grated

Preheat oven to 375°. Melt 2 tablespoons butter in a saucepan and stir in the flour. Continue stirring and cook 2 minutes. Stir in the fish or clam broth. Remove the sauce from the heat and beat in the remaining 5 tablespoons butter, a little bit at a time. Beat in the egg yolks, and continue beating until cool. Add the lemon juice and cayenne. Spoon a bit of the sauce into shells or ramekins. Divide the crabmeat, which has been picked over to check for shell, into the ramekins, and cover with the remaining sauce. Sprinkle with grated Parmesan. Bake 5 to 10 minutes until bubbling and golden brown. Glaze at the last minute under the broiler if necessary.

CREAMED OYSTERS ON HOT RICE

Serves 6 to 8.

1	quart fresh oysters
¼	cup butter
3	tablespoons flour
2	cups half & half
1	teaspoon salt
½	teaspoon curry powder
¼	teaspoon ground pepper
	Dash of paprika
2	tablespoons sherry
1	tablespoon Worcestershire sauce
1	teaspoon lemon juice
4	cups hot buttered rice
2	tablespoons minced parsley

Drain the oysters and reserve the liquid. Melt the butter in a heavy saucepan and stir in the flour. Cook for 2 minutes, then slowly add the oyster liquid and the half & half. Stir in the salt, curry powder, pepper, and paprika, and continue stirring until mixture is smooth and thick. Add the drained oysters. Bring just to the boiling point, then lower heat and simmer for 15 to 20 minutes. Remove from the heat and stir in the sherry, Worcestershire, and lemon juice. Serve over hot buttered rice or in the middle of a rice ring. Sprinkle with parsley.

Breads and Stuffings

CHEESE BISCUIT

This recipe comes from Mrs. Renshaw, a neighbor in Huntington. It is an alternative to Cheese Straws as an accompaniment to cocktails.

1   pound butter
1   pound cake flour
1   pound sharp Cheddar cheese, grated
1   teaspoon salt
     Several dashes Tabasco sauce
1   egg yolk
1   tablespoon milk
     Pecan halves

Cream the butter. Add flour slowly, then the other ingredients and mix will. Roll out about ¼ inch thick, and cut with a small cutter of any desired shape. Lightly beat the egg yolk with the milk and glaze the biscuits with the mixture. Place a pecan half in the center of each biscuit. Bake at 400° for about 10 minutes.

This dough will keep for a week or more in the refrigerator. After baking, the biscuits will keep well in a tin.

Beaten Biscuits

This is one of Gran's recipes from Mrs. Gwinn, a neighbor in Huntington. She says "to test when done, pinch sides of biscuit; if they are stiff and hold shape, biscuits are finished."

4   cups flour, measured before sifting

1   teaspoon baking powder

½   cup whole milk, cold

½   cup cold water

1   teaspoon salt

2   teaspoons sugar

¼   cup cold vegetable shortening

Preheat oven to 450°. Sift the flour with the baking powder. Mix the cold milk and water, and in it dissolve the salt and sugar. Work the shortening into the flour. Gradually add the liquid. Turn the dough onto a pastry board or marble slab and beat it with a wooden mallet until it is smooth and glossy. Continue folding the dough over and beating it for about 30 minutes. The dough will blister and pop loudly. When sufficiently blistered, the dough will be very white. Roll out to about ½ inch. Take care not to roll it too thin as beaten biscuits do not rise much. Cut with a biscuit cutter and prick each several times with a fork. Put into the oven on an ungreased cookie sheet and immediately reduce temperature to 400°. Bake for about 25 minutes.

Sally Lunn

This is best when served hot with lots of butter, but is also delicious toasted. This is a traditional southern bread made from an egg batter somewhat like a brioche.

2	cups whole milk
1	cake yeast, or 1 package dry
1	tablespoon sugar
4	tablespoons butter, melted
4	cups sifted flour
2	eggs, slightly beaten
1	teaspoon salt

Scald the milk and let it cool to lukewarm. Stir in sugar and yeast, until yeast dissolves. Add melted butter, flour, beaten eggs and salt. Beat mixture until it is smooth and bubbling. Pour into a well greased tube pan. Cover and let rise until double in bulk, about 2 hours. Meanwhile, preheat the oven to 400°. Bake the bread for 20 minutes at 400°, then reduce heat to 350° and bake 30 minutes longer, or until done.

BOLO BREAD

2 medium size loaves.

A fragrant cinnamon sweet bread.

BREAD

2	cups whole milk
1	cake yeast or 1 package dry
1½	teaspoons salt
½	cup sugar
7	cups flour
4	tablespoons butter, softened
4	tablespoons vegetable shortening
1	teaspoon salt
2	eggs, well beaten

Heat the milk and let it cool to lukewarm. Add the yeast, salt, sugar, and 2 cups of flour. Let the mixture rise until light and full of bubbles. Stir in the softened butter, shortening, remaining teaspoon salt and the 2 eggs. Add the remaining flour, about 5 cups, until it makes a soft dough. Rub the dough with vegetable shortening and put into a greased bowl, letting it rise again in a warm place. When double in bulk, divide the dough in half, and roll out each half gently on a floured board.

FILLING

4	tablespoons softened butter
	Cinnamon to taste (about 1 tablespoon total)
½	cup (heaping) light brown sugar
1	cup whole blanched almonds (or chop if you prefer)
1	cup mixed nuts, chopped (pecans and English walnuts, or your preference)
1	cup raisins, warmed slightly

Spread each half of the rolled out dough with the softened butter. Sprinkle with cinnamon, brown sugar, nuts, and raisins. Roll up like a jelly roll and cut into ½ inch slices. Lay slices cut side down in a greased bread pan in layers. On each layer sprinkle with more cinnamon. Two layers usually fill one bread pan. Continue until all the dough is used. Let rise again and bake at 350° for 40 to 45 minutes, or until it tests done with a toothpick.

Tsoureki – Greek Holiday Bread

4 loaves.

I am so flattered that Aunt Matina allowed me to share her wonderful recipe here. This makes a most delicious sweet and eggy loaf.

- ⌣ tablespoons dry yeast
- ½ cup warm water
- 1½ cups milk, scalded
- 1½ sticks butter
- 1⅛ cups sugar
- 2½ pounds all-purpose flour
- 5 eggs, room temperature
- 2 teaspoons salt
- 1 egg yolk
- 1 tablespoon whole milk
- Sesame seeds

In a small bowl, add the yeast to the warm water and let it proof. Scald the milk and pour it into a large mixing bowl. Allow the butter to melt in the hot milk. Mix the sugar with 2 cups of the flour. When the milk mixture has cooled, but is still warm, beat into it the 5 whole eggs. Add the yeast mixture, the sugar/flour mixture, and the salt, beating well. Gradually add in the remaining flour. This is easiest done initially in a heavy duty mixer while it is still sticky. As you add more of the flour you will need to pull the dough out of the bowl and knead it by hand. When it is thoroughly kneaded and elastic, put it into a large warm bowl. Cover with plastic wrap and a towel, and set it in a warm place to rise. This will take 2 to 3 hours. Punch the dough down and divide into 4 equal pieces. Place each into a warm greased loaf pan. Cover and let rise again until they are about ½ inch above the pans. Mix the egg yolk and milk well and brush this glaze on to the loaves. Sprinkle with sesame seeds if desired, and bake at 350° for about 35 minutes. If it begins to become too brown, lay foil over the top.

Oyster Stuffing

Enough for a 10-pound turkey.

1	pint oysters
2	teaspoons salt
½	teaspoon coarsely ground pepper
2	quarts dry bread crumbs
½	cup butter, melted
1-1½	cups oyster liquor

The oysters may be left whole or chopped or finely ground. Combine all ingredients and stuff the bird.

Other seasonings may be added to taste, but this stuffing retains all the delicate flavoring.

Vegetables and Grains

Georgia Beans

Serves 8.

1½	pounds green beans
2-3	slices bacon
¼	cup minced onion
1	cup cider vinegar
½	cup sugar
	Salt and pepper to taste

Leave the green beans whole or French them as you prefer, and cook them until tender in boiling salted water. Cut the bacon into small pieces and fry until crisp. Add the minced onion and cook until soft. Mix the vinegar and sugar and add to the bacon fat in the skillet. Let heat thoroughly, but do not boil. Pour over the beans with the bits of bacon and salt and pepper to taste as needed.

Spinach Parmesan

Serves 6.

3 pounds fresh spinach
6 tablespoons grated Parmesan cheese
6 tablespoons minced onion
6 tablespoons heavy cream
5 tablespoons melted butter
½ cup soft fresh bread crumbs

Wash the spinach several times and chop as fine as you want. Leave some of the water on the leaves and put into a large saucepan. Cover and cook over medium heat for 8 to 10 minutes. Drain if necessary. Mix the spinach with the cheese, onion, cream and 4 tablespoons of the butter and turn into a baking dish. Melt the remaining butter and mix well with the bread crumbs. Sprinkle over the spinach and bake at 450° for 10 to 15 minutes.

Best Beets

Serves 6.

These have a beautiful color and tangy flavor.

1 pound fresh beets
¾ tablespoon flour
½ cup sugar
¼ teaspoon salt
½ cup cider vinegar
2 tablespoons butter

Cook the beets until tender. Cool, peel and slice. You should have 2 cups. Set the beets aside, keeping them warm. In a large sauce pan, mix the flour, sugar, and salt well. Add the vinegar slowly. Whisk briefly if you have lumps of flour. Let the mixture come to a boil, stirring constantly. Cook for 5 minutes, then beat in the butter. Pour the sauce over the beets and serve hot.

Corn Pudding

Serves 6.

2   eggs, slightly beaten
1½   tablespoons melted butter
2   cups whole milk, scalded
1   teaspoon salt
⅛   teaspoon pepper
2   cups fresh corn, cut from the cob

Preheat oven to 400°. Mix together the eggs, butter, milk and seasoning. Gently stir in the corn. Turn into a butter baking dish. Bake for about 30 minutes until firm.

Sweet Potato Soufflé

Serves 6 to 8.

3   cups mashed cooked sweet potato
1   tablespoon butter, melted
1   cup whole milk
2   eggs, separated
⅔   cup sugar (or less if desired)
1   teaspoon salt
1   teaspoon nutmeg
1   teaspoon cinnamon
⅓   cup chopped pecans (optional)
⅓   cup raisins (optional)

Preheat the oven to 350°. In a large bowl stir the mashed cooked sweet potato with the butter, milk, and egg yolks. Add the sugar and spices. Stir in the pecans and raisins if desired. Beat the egg whites until stiff, but not dry, and fold into the sweet potato mixture. Turn into a buttered soufflé dish or casserole and bake for about 1 hour.

Fruits

BAKED BANANAS

This is one of my children's favorite dishes. It is a delicious accompaniment to roast chicken, duck or ham. You will need to serve it as a side dish in its own bowl with the sauce spooned over it.

6	tablespoons butter
¾	cup sugar
6	tablespoons lemon juice
½	cup orange juice
12	small bananas (slightly underripe is best)

Preheat the oven to 350°. Place butter, sugar and fruit juices in a pan over low heat until the butter is melted. Spread the peeled bananas in a shallow baking dish and pour the sauce over them. Bake for 30 minutes, basting frequently.

BAKED FRUITS

Serves 6.

This is a divine side dish especially with poultry or ham. I've included just a few of the many fruit side dishes in our family repertoire. I don't know why we don't serve them more!

1	cup light brown sugar
3	tablespoons flour
3	large firm tart apples
3	oranges
1	grapefruit
1	teaspoon grated lemon rind
4	tablespoons butter

Preheat the oven to 400°. Mix the sugar and the flour together and set aside. Peel all the fruit, core the apples, and cut fruit into thick slices (or rings for the apples). In a deep 8-inch casserole, put a layer of grapefruit, a layer of orange, then a layer of apple. Between each layer put ½ teaspoon grated lemon rind, about ½ cup of the brown sugar and flour mixture and dot with butter. Repeat the layers, ending on top with the apple rings. Bake for 1½ hours.

Apples in Maple Syrup

When cooked at low temperature, the apples keep their shape. They are tender and turn a rich, deep red. This is delicious with ham, duck, or chicken.

2	quarts Winesap apples (if you can't find Winesaps, try York, Cortland, or Rome)
1½	cups real maple syrup
1	lemon, cut in very thin slices
3	tablespoons butter

Pare and core apples and cut them into eighths. Add to them the maple syrup and the thin lemon slices. Turn into a shallow earthenware or ceramic baking dish, large enough to hold everything. Dot heavily with butter. Bake covered for 4 hours at 350° or for 6 hours at 300°.

Preserves and Conserves

Superb Blackberry Jam

About 1½ pints.

3-4	pints blackberries
2½	cups sugar

Set aside 1½ cups whole blackberries. Purée the remaining blackberries and strain out the seeds. You should have 2 cups of pulp. In a heavy pan, put the pulp and an equal amount of sugar. Let the mixture come to a boil and add ½ additional cup of sugar. Let boil 5 minutes and add the reserved berries. Let the mixture boil about 15 minutes more until it is thick and the drops run together on the edge of a kitchen spoon and sheet off. (This takes some practice to know when it is done.) Skim the jam as it is cooking so that you remove all of the white foam. When the jam tests done, pour into sterilized half pint jars immediately and process in a water bath.

Superb Red Raspberry Jam

About 1½ pints.

These jams must be made in small batches. I usually do several batches at a time, starting my kettles about 10 minutes apart.

3-4   pints red raspberries
3   cups sugar

Set aside 1 heaping pint whole raspberries. Purée the remaining raspberries and strain out the seeds. You should have 2 cups of pulp. In a heavy pan, put the pulp and an equal amount of sugar. Let the mixture come to a boil and add 1 additional cup of sugar. Let boil 5 minutes and add the reserved raspberries. Let the mixture boil about 15 minutes more until it is thick and the drops run together on the edge of a kitchen spoon and sheet off. Skim the jam as it is cooking so that you remove all of the white foam. When the jam tests done, pour into sterilized half pint jars immediately and process in a water bath.

I have a wonderful attachment for my Kitchen Aid mixer that purées and strains the raspberry pulp. You can also do it in the food processor and strain through a sieve.

Marvelous Strawberry Preserves

About 1 to 1½ pints.

3   cups strawberries
2   cups sugar
1½   tablespoons lemon juice

Wash the berries and cut them in half if they are large. Put the in a heavy kettle and add the sugar and lemon juice. Cook slowly over a low flame until the sugar dissolves completely. Then boil over a higher heat until the syrup is thick and sheets from the spoon. This takes about 15 to 20 minutes. Watch constantly and skim off the white foam. Stir frequently. Pour immediately into sterilized jars and seal while hot. Process in a water bath.

Best Peach Jam

About 2 pints.

This makes a delicious jam of a beautiful color as the peaches have a rosy red skin.

2-3   pounds freestone peaches

2½-3 cups sugar

2   tablespoons orange juice

1   tablespoon lemon juice

1   teaspoon vanilla

Wash the peaches well, cut out any blemishes, but do not skin them. Quarter the fruit and grind, skin-on, with a coarse grinding disk on your heavy duty mixer if you have one. If you do not, use a food processor. You need 2 cups of pulp. Put the pulp into a heavy kettle with the orange and lemon juices. Bring the mixture to a boil and simmer slowly until transparent and thick. This takes about 15 minutes after it comes to a boil. Skim off the white foam as it cooks. Stir often as this jam is likely to stick. Cook until it is thick and sheets from a spoon. Take it from the heat and add the vanilla. Pour into sterilized jars and seal while hot. Process in a hot water bath.

Fig and Lemon Jam

This is a delightful way to use up Charleston's ubiquitous figs during the summer months. A small piece of stem ginger is nice to cook with this jam.

3   pounds ripe figs

1½   pounds sugar

1   lemon, sliced very thin, seeds discarded

Cut figs in pieces and put in a heavy kettle. Add the sugar and lemon slices, mixing well. Place on low heat until the sugar is dissolved. Bring to a boil, then lower the heat again and simmer until the jam is thick. Stir often to prevent burning. Pour into hot sterile jars and seal at once. Process in a hot water bath.

GRAN'S CHUTNEY

2½ pints.

This chutney is fabulous and makes a wonderful gift.

WEIGHT OF ALL FRUIT AFTER BEING PREPARED:

¾	pound tart apples, peeled, cored, and cut into sixteenths
1	pound peaches, skinned and sliced
¼	pound dried apricots
½	cup raisins
1	small onion, chopped
¼	cup chopped fresh mint leaves
3-4	large roots of preserved ginger, sliced thin
2	tablespoons syrup from preserved ginger
1	teaspoon ground cinnamon
½	teaspoon ground cloves
¼	teaspoon mace
¼	teaspoon allspice
2	teaspoons salt
1	tablespoon chili powder
½	teaspoon dried mustard
1	pound dark brown sugar
1	pint cider vinegar

Peel and slice the apples and peaches before weighing them. Put them in a large, heavy kettle and add the other ingredients, mixing well. Cook over low heat for about 2½ hours until the mixture is very thick. Seal at once in sterile jars and process in a water bath.

Russian Apple Conserve

This recipe comes from Mrs. Bashkiroff, whom my grandparents knew in New York. The story Gran told was that "somehow her smart cookie of a son had gotten her out of Russia. He had made millions and married a beautiful, beautiful, Russian wife, twenty years younger than he. Mrs. Bashkiroff ran the house and cooked."

1½	pounds firm, tart apples (Winesaps, Romes, or Cortlands)
2	cups sugar
1	cup water
3	strips lemon peel
½	vanilla bean

Peel the apples and cut them into sixteenths, reserving the apple peel. In a very heavy kettle make a syrup of the sugar and water and add the lemon peel and the apple peels. Bring to a boil, and let it boil 5 minutes. Skim and remove peelings. Add the apple slices and the half vanilla bean which has been cut into small pieces. Cook for 1 hour over very low heat. Cover the kettle for the first 30 minutes. Cool and store in the refrigerator, or seal in jars while hot and process. Let stand 24 hours before using.

It is critical to get the right kind of apple for this dish—one that will hold its shape through cooking. This is a marvelous side dish. The apple slices are translucent and the syrup jells slightly. This is most delicious with ham, chicken, duck, or any birds, or simply as a preserve on toast.

Desserts

Mother's Pecan Cake

This recipe comes from my great-grandmother Wiles.

½   cup good brandy

1   whole nutmeg

1   pound raisins

2   cups butter, softened

2   cups sugar

10 eggs, separated

4½ cups cake flour

1   teaspoon baking powder

½   teaspoon salt

1½ pounds pecans, chopped coarsely

¼   pound citron, chopped into small pieces
    (optional)

Soak the nutmeg in the brandy overnight. Soak the raisins in the brandy for about an hour. Preheat the oven to 350°. Cream the butter thoroughly. Add the sugar, and cream until light and fluffy. Add the egg yolks and beat well. Sift the flour with the baking powder and salt. Add flour mixture gradually to the butter and sugar, alternating with the brandy from which the nutmeg has been removed. Mix well. Stir in the raisins and pecans. Beat the egg whites until stiff, but not dry. Fold into the butter and flour mixture. Bake in a greased and floured 10-inch tube pan for 1 hour or until a toothpick in the center comes out clean. Cool on a rack and dust with powdered sugar.

BLACKBERRY CAKE

1	cup butter, softened
2	cups light brown sugar
6	eggs, separated
3	cups cake flour
2	teaspoons baking soda
2	teaspoons ground cinnamon
1	teaspoon ground allspice
1	teaspoon ground nutmeg
1	cup sour cream
1	cup seedless blackberry jam

Preheat oven to 350°. Cream butter thoroughly. Add the sugar and cream together until light and fluffy. Blend in the egg yolks. Sift the flour with the soda and spices, and add it to the butter mixture alternately with the sour cream. Mix in the jam, blending well. Beat the egg whites until stiff but not dry, and fold into the mixture. Bake in a greased and floured 10-inch tube pan for one hour or longer until a toothpick inserted comes out clean. Cover with Seven Minute Frosting or any good icing.

DELICIOUS SPICE CAKE

This fragrant spice cake comes from Mrs. Meek from Huntington who was known for her wonderful cakes.

¾	cup butter, softened
2	scant cups granulated sugar
3	eggs
3	scant cups cake flour
2	teaspoons baking powder
1	teaspoon ground cinnamon
½	teaspoon ground cloves
½	teaspoon ground allspice
¼	teaspoon ground nutmeg
1	cup whole milk
1	teaspoon vanilla

Preheat oven to 350°. Cream the butter and add the sugar, creaming thoroughly. Add the egg yolks, one at a time, and beat well after each addition. Sift the cake flour with the baking powder and spices, and add to the butter mixture alternately with the milk. Stir in the vanilla. Beat the egg whites until stiff, but not dry, and fold into the batter. Pour into a greased and floured 10-inch tube pan. Bake for 50 to 60 minutes, or until it tests done. Ice with Seven Minute Icing or any good boiled white icing.

MOTHER'S BEST DEVIL'S FOOD CAKE

A recipe from my great-grandmother.

1	cup butter, softened
2	cups granulated sugar
4	eggs, separated and at room temperature
2½	cups cake flour
1½	teaspoons baking powder
1	teaspoon baking soda
3	ounces unsweetened chocolate
2	teaspoons vanilla
1	cup buttermilk

Preheat the oven to 350°. Grease and flour two 8- or 9-inch round pans (or see next page if using for Ice Box Cake). Melt the chocolate and set aside. Cream the butter and add the sugar and the egg yolks. Beat well. Sift the cake flour with the baking powder and soda. Add it gradually to the butter mixture, alternately with the buttermilk. Stir in the melted chocolate. Beat the egg whites until stiff, but not dry, and fold into the batter last. Pour into the two prepared pans and bake about 30 minutes or until they test done.

CHOCOLATE BUTTERCREAM ICING

Enough for 1 double-layer cake.

This was my great-grandmother's recipe for chocolate icing. Use it on her Devil's Food cake if you are making the cake alone and not for the Ice Box Cake.

¼	pound butter, softened
2	cups powdered sugar
4	tablespoons cocoa powder
4	tablespoons boiling water or strong coffee
2	teaspoons vanilla

Cream the butter and add the powdered sugar, creaming well. Melt the cocoa in the boiling water or coffee, and mix until smooth. Add to the butter and sugar, mixing well. Lastly, stir in the vanilla. Beat all until thoroughly blended and smooth.

Chocolate Ice Box Cake

Serves 12.

Base

Bake a thin layer of Devil's Food Cake in a 9-inch spring form pan and let it cool on a rack. When cool, replace it in the pan. Alternatively, you may use a layer of crushed almond macaroons.

Filling

½	pound butter, softened
1	pound powdered sugar
4	eggs, separated
1	teaspoon vanilla
2	ounces unsweetened chocolate, melted
¼	pound blanched slivered almonds (optional)

Cream butter with sugar and add the egg yolks, blending until smooth. Add the vanilla and melted chocolate, mixing well. Beat the egg whites until stiff but not dry, and fold into the butter mixture. Stir in almonds if you want to use them.

Assembly

1	package ladyfingers, split in half
1	cup heavy cream, whipped stiff
2	tablespoons powdered sugar (optional)
¼	teaspoon vanilla (optional)

In the springform pan with the Devil's Food Cake or crushed macaroons in the bottom, line the sides with the ladyfinger halves. Pour the chocolate mixture into the center and let refrigerate for several hours or overnight. Whip the cream and stir in the powdered sugar and vanilla if you wish. Take the sides off the pan and fill it with the whipped cream.

It is easier to serve if the cake is cut in slices after the filling is hard, but before adding the whipped cream. I prefer the silky smooth chocolate without the nuts, but the chocolate and almond combination is also wonderful.

CINNAMON CUPCAKES WITH CHOCOLATE ICING

This recipe comes from Mrs. Hazel Sharpnack, a good friend of my great-grandmother's from Huntington.

CAKE

½	cup butter, softened
1	cup granulated sugar
2	eggs, separated
1½	cups cake flour
2½	teaspoons baking powder
1	tablespoon ground cinnamon
	Pinch of salt
½	cup whole milk
½	teaspoon vanilla

Preheat the oven to 350°. Cream butter and add sugar, creaming together well. Add the egg yolks one at a time, beating well after each addition. Sift the cake flour with the baking powder, cinnamon and salt, and add gradually to the butter mixture, alternately with the milk. Stir in the vanilla. Beat the egg whites until they are stiff, but not dry, and fold into the batter. Line 18 to 20 (2½-inch) muffin cups with paper liners. Pour in the batter. It should fill the cup by about ⅔. Bake for 15 to 20 minutes or until they test done. Cool on a rack and ice with Chocolate Frosting below.

CHOCOLATE FROSTING

2	cups sugar
1	cup heavy cream
3	ounces unsweetened chocolate
	Pinch of salt
2	ounces butter
1	teaspoon vanilla

In a heavy saucepan, put the sugar, cream, chocolate and salt. Cook over low heat until the sugar dissolves, and stir until the chocolate is melted and the ingredients are smooth and well mixed. Continue stirring over low heat until a candy thermometer has reached the softball stage. Remove from heat and add butter and vanilla. As it cools, beat until it is thick and creamy, then ice cooled Cinnamon Cupcakes.

CARAMEL CAKE

In our family this cake is known as "Devilish Thing" because it's so hard to resist. The frosting is terribly rich—almost like fudge candy, and it's hard to stop taking just "one more finger" as Gran used to say.

WHITE CAKE

1	cup butter, softened
2	cups granulated sugar
3	cups sifted cake flour
1	tablespoon baking powder
1	cup whole milk
1	teaspoon vanilla
	Pinch of salt
6	egg whites at room temperature

Preheat oven to 350°. Grease and flour two 8- or 9-inch square pans. Cream the butter, add the sugar and cream again thoroughly. Sift the cake flour with the baking powder, and add gradually to the butter mixture alternately with the milk. Stir in the vanilla. Beat the egg whites with the salt until it forms peaks that are stiff, but not dry. Fold into the batter. Pour into the prepared pans and bake about 30 minutes or until it tests done. Cool on a rack and ice each layer as a single layer cake with Caramel Frosting below. You can also make it as one sheet cake.

CARAMEL FROSTING

¾	cup butter
1½	cups light brown sugar, firmly packed
¼	teaspoon salt
⅓	cup whole milk
1	pound (3½ cups) powdered sugar, sifted
½	teaspoon vanilla
	Cream as needed

Melt the butter in a large heavy saucepan. Add the brown sugar and salt and cook over low heat about 2 minutes, stirring constantly. Add the milk and continue stirring until the mixture comes to a boil. Remove from heat and gradually beat in the powdered sugar. You may need to use a hand-held electric beater or a whisk for a minute if it has lumps. Stir in the vanilla and mix well. Thin with a small amount of cream if the frosting is too stiff to spread easily. (I never find this necessary.) Spread while still warm on each layer of the white cake.

WOODFORD PUDDING

This is an old fashioned favorite Kentucky dessert, popular for many years. Serve it with Pudding Sauce, below.

½	cup butter, softened
¾	cup granulated sugar
3	eggs, separated
1	cup seedless blackberry jam
¾	cup all-purpose flour
2	teaspoons baking powder
1	teaspoon ground cinnamon
¼	teaspoon ground cloves
½	teaspoon ground nutmeg
¼	teaspoon ground allspice
2	tablespoons heavy cream

Preheat the oven to 325°. Grease and flour a 10-inch tube pan and set it aside. Cream the butter and add the sugar, mixing well. Add the egg yolks one at a time, beating after each addition. Add the blackberry jam, mixing thoroughly. Sift the flour with the baking powder and spices, then add it gradually to the batter, alternating with the cream. Beat the egg whites until they are stiff, but not dry, and fold into the batter. Pour into the prepared pan and bake for 40 minutes or until a toothpick inserted in the center comes out dry, as for any cake.

PUDDING SAUCE

⅓	cup butter
⅓	cup sugar
2	egg yolks
3	tablespoons cognac
⅓	cup heavy cream, whipped

Melt the butter in the top of a double boiler. Stir in the sugar, and continue stirring until it is dissolved. Beat the egg yolks and add them one at a time to the butter/sugar mixture. Cook over hot water until it begins to thicken. Do not boil. Cool it and add the cognac and whipped cream just before serving.

For use with another pudding you may substitute 2 tablespoons lemon juice and 1 tablespoon finely grated lemon rind for the cognac.

173

Graham Cracker Pudding

This is not a pudding in the sense we use the term today, but rather a cake.

Cake

½	cup butter, softened
1	cup sugar
1	cup whole milk
2	eggs, separated
1¾	cups graham cracker crumbs
½	cup flour*
2	teaspoons baking powder
	Pinch of salt
½	cup pecans, very coarsely chopped

Preheat oven to 375°. Cream butter and sugar. Add milk and egg yolks, blending well. Mix the graham cracker crumbs, flour (if you are using it), baking powder, and salt, and add gradually to the butter mixture. Stir in the pecans. Beat the egg whites until stiff but not dry, and fold into the mixture. Pour into 2 (9-inch) cake pans which have been greased and floured. Bake for 25 to 30 minutes, or until it tests done.

Two cups of graham cracker crumbs may be substituted for the crumb/flour mixture.

Filling

1	cup heavy cream, whipped
2	tablespoons powdered sugar

Whip the cream and sweeten if desired with the sugar.

Assembly

Turn the cake layers out of the pans and cool on a rack. Put the sweetened whipped cream between the layers and serve with Caramel Sauce.

CARAMEL SAUCE

1	tablespoon butter
2	cups light brown sugar, or a mixture of light and dark
3	egg yolks
1	cup whole milk
1	teaspoon vanilla

Melt the butter in the top of a double boiler. Stir in the brown sugar, then the milk, mixing thoroughly. Add the egg yolks and blend well. Cook in the top of a double boiler until as thick as very heavy cream. Remove from heat and add vanilla. Serve over Graham Cracker Pudding.

SEVEN MINUTE ICING

Enough to cover 2 (9-inch) layers.

This is an all-purpose icing which can be used on the Blackberrry Cake, Spice Cake and others. It does not keep well.

2	egg whites, at room temperature
¼	teaspoon cream of tartar
	Pinch of salt
1½	cups granulated sugar
5	tablespoons cold water
1½	teaspoons light corn syrup
1	teaspoon vanilla

Put the egg whites, cream of tartar, sugar, water, and corn syrup in the top part of a double boiler. Beat with a hand-held mixer until thoroughly mixed. Place over rapidly boiling water and beat constantly for 7 minutes, until the icing will stand in peaks. Remove from the heat. Add the vanilla and continue beating until the icing has cooled and is thick enough to spread.

Flakey Pie Crust

This makes 2 (9- or 10-inch) pie shells.

2½   cups flour

½   teaspoon salt

1   cup shortening (I prefer a mixture of ⅓ butter and ⅔ vegetable shortening)

6   tablespoons ice water

In a large bowl, stir the salt into the flour and use a pastry blender to cut the shortening into the flour until it resembles coarse meal. Add ice water and mix well until the dough pulls together into a ball. Divide the dough in half, pat each half out into a round, and wrap in wax paper. Refrigerate for 30 minutes before rolling out and lining the pie pan. Fill with desired filling and bake as instructed.

To prepare in a food processor, add flour and salt to the processor bowl. Add the shortening and pulse until it resembles coarse meal. Add the ice water and pulse again until it barely comes together. Divide and refrigerate. To blind-bake a crust, line the pie pan with the crust and prick it all over with a fork. Line the crust with a square of waxed paper or parchment and fill it with dried rice or beans to weight it down. Bake in a preheated oven for 10 minutes at 400°. Remove the rice or beans and return the pie shell to the oven for about 15 minutes or until it is a golden brown. Cool it on a rack until ready to fill.

Old Fashioned Pound Cake

1   pound butter, softened

1   pound sugar

10   large eggs

½   teaspoon ground mace

2   tablespoons brandy

1   pound cake flour, sifted twice

1   teaspoon baking powder

¼   teaspoon salt

Preheat the oven to 325°. Cream butter and sugar thoroughly. Add the eggs one at a time, beating between additions. Add the mace and the brandy. Sift the flour with the baking powder and salt and gradually add it to the butter mixture. Grease a 12-cup Bundt pan or a 10-inch tube pan well and flour it. Bake for 1 hour or until it tests done.

Butterscotch Pie

Filling

¾	cup butter
½	cup flour
1½	cups light brown sugar
3	egg yolks
1½	cups whole milk
¼	teaspoon salt

Prepare and bake a pie shell and set aside. Melt butter in the top of a double boiler. Add flour, stirring, and cook for about 2 minutes. Add brown sugar, egg yolks, milk and salt and mix well. Continue to cook, stirring constantly until the mixture is thick and smooth, about 15 minutes. Let cool for 15 to 30 minutes, and pour into the prepared shell.

Top with Brown Sugar Meringue or with whipped cream.

Brown Sugar Meringue

3	egg whites at room temperature
¼	teaspoon salt (scant)
¼	teaspoon cream of tartar
5	tablespoons light brown sugar
½	teaspoon vanilla

In an electric mixer, beat egg whites and salt until foamy. Add cream of tartar and continue beating at high speed until soft peaks form. Gradually add brown sugar, one tablespoon at a time, until it forms stiff peaks. Add vanilla last. Top pie with meringue and bake at 350° for 15 minutes or until meringue is golden. Serve at room temperature or chilled.

Another variation is to top with whipped cream and cover with grated coconut. This is a wonderful and very rich pie.

PEACH DUMPLINGS

6	peaches
1	pint water
1	cup granulated sugar
2	tablespoons butter
1	batch Flakey Pie Crust (see page 176)

Preheat oven to 350°. Peel peaches and wrap each in a square of thinly rolled Flakey Pie Crust. Arrange the peaches in a shallow oven-proof baking dish. Meanwhile, in a medium saucepan, make a syrup of the water, sugar, and butter. Pour the syrup around the peaches and bake for 30 to 45 minutes. Serve with Grandmother Wiles' Sauce for Dumplings (Chapter VIII).

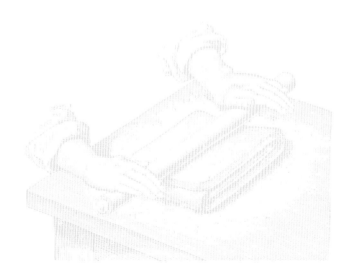

COUSIN CORINNE'S KENTUCKY CREAM CANDY

¼ pound butter

1 pint heavy cream

1 cup water

6 cups granulated sugar

¼ teaspoon salt

¼ teaspoon soda

1 teaspoon vanilla

In a very large, heavy kettle, put the butter. As it begins to melt, add the cream and water. Measure the sugar exactly, and add the salt and soda to it, mixing well. Add to the butter and cream mixture. Stir until well blended. Do not stir again after just mixing the ingredients. Wash the sugar crystals off the side of the pan occasionally with a pastry brush dipped in water. Let it cook over low heat for about 1 hour until it reaches the hard ball stage on a candy thermometer. It will be golden in color. Grease a marble slab with butter, and pour the mixture quickly onto it. Do not scrape the bottom or sides of the pan. Continually turn the edges of the mixture into the center as it cools. When it is cool enough to handle, pull it for half an hour over a candy hook or with another person. Always pull with the same twist and in the same direction. If your hands become too hot, dip them from time to time in cold water. Continue to pull until the candy begins to turn white or cream-colored. Twist it into a rope about 1 to 1½ inches thick and cut into pieces. As soon as it does not stick together, put it in a tightly covered tin with waxed paper between the layers. Let it stand overnight and it will cream. You may serve it plain, or dip it in melted semi-sweet chocolate.

This must be made in cool weather, and will keep for a long time if each piece is wrapped in waxed paper. Be careful not to allow sugar crystals to form, or the candy will be ruined. This makes an enormous batch. You may want to cut it in half.

For the Freezer

Thank those clever engineers for the deep freeze, or I could never have managed such a party with house guests and tours, etc. We had fixed my dish of chicken breasts, boned, with white wine, mushrooms, and sour cream added at the last—did it all Monday. We had a Virginia ham, a lettuce and avocado salad, and the pecan roll with caramel sauce.

~ JWS – 4/5/69

One of the keys to Gran's frequent entertaining, for large and small events alike, was her constant replenishment of party foods in her freezer. Her letters, notes, and party books are full of references to the elements of the menu which were prepared ahead and frozen. She always had an extra freezer in the household, and spent many days preparing desserts, soups, stocks, and sauces which could then be pulled out at a moment's notice and assembled along with fresh items into a delicious meal.

These are some of her particular recommendations for the freezer:

Sauce Supreme – This is used for crêpes, chicken dishes, etc. (see Chicken Breasts in Sauce Supreme). Prepare and freeze until needed.

Beef Stock – Freeze and use for vegetable soups.

Chicken Breasts in White Wine – complete the dish and freeze until ready to use.

Blanquette of Veal – complete up to the point of adding cream, then freeze until ready to use.

Pie and Tart Shells – Prepare the dough and assemble in pie or tart tins. They can be frozen until needed for pies, tarts, or quiches.

Pumpkin Pie – Prepare completely and freeze before baking. See recipe for instructions on baking a frozen pumpkin pie.

Orange Cake – This can be prepared and frozen in a ring mold of desired size, or in a loaf. Defrost the cake and ice or glaze it when ready to serve. Serve with ice cream or sherbet in the center and sauce on the side.

Mrs. Hazel's Cinnamon Cake – Freeze in ring mold or as cupcakes. Defrost, then ice with chocolate icing or serve with a chocolate ice cream and dark bittersweet chocolate sauce.

Mrs. Meek's Spice Cake – Freezes well. Just defrost and ice with seven-minute frosting when ready to serve.

Mother's Marble Cake – Freezes perfectly and can be served warm or at room temperature.

Chocolate Dessert Roll – Prepare and roll with plain, mocha, or peppermint stick whipped cream. Freeze. Defrost in the refrigerator until cake and whipped cream are softened. Serve with a hot chocolate sauce.

Pecan Dessert Roll – Freeze as above with whipped cream rolled inside. Defrost and serve with warm caramel sauce.

Crêpes – As noted in the recipe for crêpes, these freeze well. Spend some time making two or three batches of crêpes, stack them between individual squares of aluminum foil, and wrap stacks of a dozen or so in heavy-duty foil before freezing. They can then be used whenever you like for dessert crêpes or main-dish meals filled with crab or chicken.

Other dishes to make ahead:

Snappy Salad Dressing – Keeps for months in the refrigerator in a Mason jar. Before using, warm to room temperature to dissolve the solidified olive oil.

Whole Cranberry Sauce – Keeps for months in the refrigerator in a Mason jar. Make for the holidays, then use throughout the year as a condiment with turkey, chicken, etc.

Pecan Tea Cakes – These keep well for two weeks in a well-sealed tin, although they never last that long!

Tante's Shortbread Cookies – These keep well for two weeks in a well-sealed tin.

I have also noted in each individual recipe where a dish can be prepared ahead and kept in refrigerator, freezer or tin until you are ready to use it.

Bibliography

Beach, Virginia Christian. *Medway*. Charleston, S.C.: Wyrick and Company, 1999.

Mouzon, Harold A. "The Carolina Art Association: Its First Hundred Years." *The South Carolina Historical Magazine* July 1958.

Pinckney, Josephine. *Three O'Clock Dinner*. New York: The Viking Press, 1945.

Rhett, Blanche S. et al. *Two Hundred Years of Charleston Cooking*. New York: Jonathan Cape & Harrison Smith, 1930.

Smith, Alice R. Huger and Herbert Ravenel Sass. *A Carolina Rice Plantation of the Fifties*. New York: William Morrow and Company, 1936.

Tannahill, Reay. *Food in History*. New York: Stein and Day, 1973.

Taylor, John Martin. *Hoppin' John's Lowcountry Cooking*. New York: Bantam Books, 1992.

The Carolina Housewife. Charleston, S.C.: Walker, Evans & Cogswell, Printers, Fifth Edition.

Verner, Elizabeth O'Neill. *Mellowed By Time*. Charleston, S.C.: Tradd Street Press, 1941.

Wootten, Bayard and Samuel Gaillard Stoney. *Charleston: Azaleas and Old Bricks*. Boston: Houghton Mifflin Company, 1939.

Index

At Home ~ Charleston

Catherine H. Forrester
P.O. Box 21493
Charleston, South Carolina 29413-1493
Telephone: 843-278-1086
Fax: 843-278-1201

Please send me:

At Home ~ Charleston   @ $28.95 each Quantity _____ $ _____

South Carolina residents add 6% sales tax   _____ $

Shipping and Handling for first book   @ $ 5.00 each $ _____

Additional books to same address   @ $ 3.00 each $ _____

                                    Total enclosed $ _____

Make check payable to *At Home ~ Charleston LLC*

Ship to:

Name _____

Address_____

City _____ State _____ Zip Code _____

Telephone_____ Email _____

Thank you for your order
For additional orders, go to www.athomecharleston.com

THE LOWCOUNTRY
of
SOUTH CAROLINA
from the ACE Basin north to Winyah Bay
including a detail of Charleston

to NORTH CAROLINA MOUNTAINS
and to HWY. 11

S.C. peaches

I-26

I-526

ASHLEY RIVER

COOPER RIVER

Charleston

FOLLY RD.

to SAVANNAH

HWY. 17

HOLLYWOOD

MAP BY: ELIZABETH PORCHER JONES

WADMALAW ISLAND

JOHNS ISLAND

JAMES ISLAND

FOLLY BEACH

ACE BASIN

ROCKVILLE

KIAWAH ISLAND

EDISTO ISLAND

SEABROOK ISLAND

ST. HELENA SOUND

EDISTO BEACH

ATLANTIC